The mystic ......'s

THE CALL OF ST. CLARE "is a love story, which though as touching as a romantic novel, is the story of a love fulfilled in God alone."

At barely seventeen, Clare Offreduccio of Assisi made an irrevocable decision—to leave a family life of wealth and position and bind herself to privation and humility in the service of God. It was a decision of love.

The splendor of Clare and her way of life is sometimes obscured by the dramatic figure of her zealous friend and confessor, Francis of Assisi. The true witnesses to Clare's spiritual perfection are her life, letters, prayers and testament, which establish her place beside Francis. Together the two saints rebuilt the crumbling Church of the thirteenth century.

Henri Daniel-Rops has gathered here the most ancient accounts and documents that deal with Clare to illumine his biography of an heroic soul. This study of a remarkable woman, friend of popes, counselor to saints, herself one of the Church's great saints, reveals the secret of a special grace . . . a grace that after seven centuries still guides her followers, the Poor Clares.

...... for our time. ...ranciscan ideal will find ....tion in this book.

...ges of magnificent photo- ...t. Here are scenes famil- ...wn of Assisi and its en- ...e convent of St. Damian, ... years. Here too are like- ...th and age, at work and ...Vivarini, Tiberus and an ...e fourteenth century.

...ANIEL-ROPS

..., journalist and novelist, ...ver to be elected to the ...d a winner of the Grand

...f published titles, which ...eventy historical studies, ...vorks of poetry and fic- ...many additional honors. ...red on him the title of ...rder of St. Gregory the ...XIII awarded him the Grand Cross.

Currently acting as editor-in-chief of THE TWENTIETH CENTURY ENCYCLOPEDIA OF CATHOLICISM, Daniel-Rops has contributed the much-acclaimed *What Is the Bible?* to the 150-volume series.

His latest success in this country is *Daily Life in the Time of Jesus.* Other Hawthorn titles by Daniel-Rops include *The Heroes of God, The Book of Mary* and *Monsieur Vincent.*

The Call of St. Clare

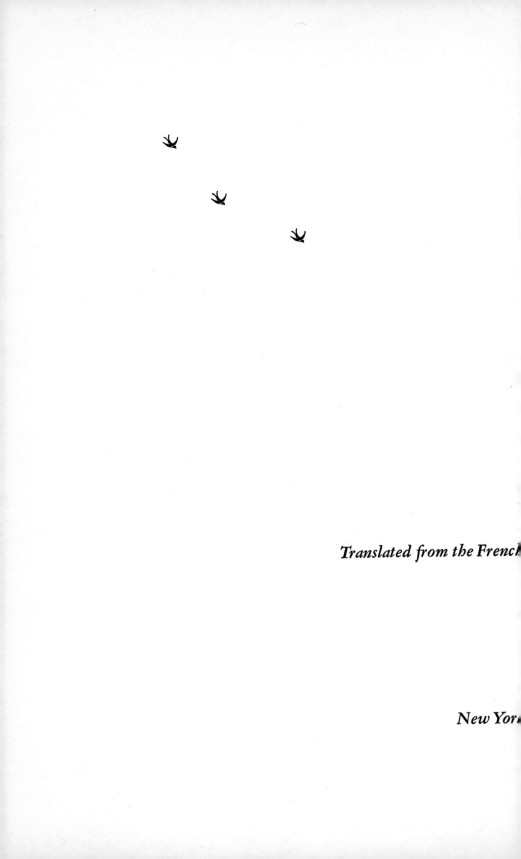

Translated from the French

New York

The Call of St. Clare

by HENRI DANIEL-ROPS

by SALVATOR ATTANASIO

HAWTHORN BOOKS, INC.   *Publishers*

FIRST EDITION
September, 1963

NIHIL OBSTAT   IMPRIMATUR
JOHN A. GOODWINE, J.C.D.   ✠ FRANCIS CARDINAL SPELLMAN
    CENSOR LIBRORUM   ARCHBISHOP OF NEW YORK
        NEW YORK, *June 14, 1963*

The *nihil obstat* and *imprimatur* are declarations that a book or pamphlet is free of doctrinal or moral error. No implication is contained therein that those who have granted the *nihil obstat* and *imprimatur* agree with the contents, opinions, or statements expressed.

H–1068

Contents

In the Light of Assisi

Text/Prayers/Testament

List of Illustrations

Illustrations 8, 9, 10, 11, 12, 15 and 17 are scenes from a painting in the basilica of St. Clare, Assisi. The work, depicting the life of St. Clare, was completed about the end of the twelfth century.

Illustrations 18, 19, 20, 21, 22, 24, 25, 27 and 29 are scenes from the convent of St. Damian, Assisi.

In the Light of Assisi

1

A love story

This is a love story which, though as touching as a romantic novel, is the story of a love fulfilled in God alone.

The night was clear and cool over the green Umbrian plain, illuminated by an almost full moon. The little town was sleeping, locked behind its ramparts, all windows dark, all doors closed. It was the evening of a beautiful Sunday, Palm Sunday, the liturgy of which, with great ceremony, had commemorated the entry of the Lord into Jerusalem and opened the holiest of all the weeks of the year.

In a dark corner of the noble house of Favarone Offreduccio, however, a frail figure was frantically engaged in an unusual task. Dressed in a heavy satin robe, embroidered in gold and trimmed with ermine, her bodice jeweled and her hair glistening with pearls, the young girl was feverishly working to remove an enormous pile of beams, broken columns, and sundry objects that were piled high in front of a closed gate: the gate of the dead which opened only to let those pass who were abandoning the house forever. Obviously she was alive—
yet she was leaving. . . .

After a long, painful, silent effort, the girl succeeded. The bolt creaked in the lock and the heavy shaft of the door turned. A shadow loomed suddenly in the chink of the door. "Is it you?" whispered the fugitive. Her faithful friend was at the rendezvous. And both, making off along the lanes intersected by stairs every stone of which was familiar, reached the end of the rampart which they knew to be poorly guarded.

They were so nervous that they could hardly keep from laughing when they found themselves on the road leading toward the plain. At seventeen it's no trifling matter to run away from home and into the country at night under an enormous moon. To the right of them, Assisi raised above its proud ramparts the irregular surfaces of its façades and terraces. Fragments of gigantic, but ruined, walls, the only remains of the castle torn down in a fury by the people of the Commune, could still be seen on the Rocca. Farther, behind them, in the purple darkness, Mount Subasio seemed a silent monster about to claw at the plain with a menacing paw. They were walking fast, not from fear but from sheer joy. And the light breeze that made the blue leaves of the olive trees rustle stroked their foreheads like a gentle, caressing hand.

Jets of warm light pierced the cold pallor of the night at the point where the path joined the road leading to the plain. Two men were standing near the turning, holding aloft blazing torches. They were dressed in brown cowls like those worn by Umbrian peasants; they seemed to be waiting for someone. When the fugitives came up to them, one of them cried out: "My soul magnifies the Lord, and my spirit rejoices in God my Savior . . ." The younger one immediately replied with the next words of the prayer, "Because he has regarded the lowliness of his handmaid . . ."

A surprising incident

An adept observer would have been aware of an event, trivial in itself but enormously rich in its significance, which had occurred on this very morning, an event which had a mysterious correlation with these doings of the night. At the High Mass in that day it was the custom for each of the worshipers walked past in procession before the Head Bishop, seated near the altar, in order to receive a palm leaf from him, blessed and censed by the bishop himself, the palm that would have a place of honor in the house for the rest of the year. When Clare's turn came to ascend the steps of the altar and kneel before the pastor, one would have seen her motionless in her place, her glance fixed above her, her features illumined by an inner joy, visibly rapt in ecstatic meditation.

Then, as her neighbor nudged her in order to rouse her attention, our observer would have seen Bishop Guido, smiling and making a sign. He rose from his chair and came down from the sanctuary, holding a palm in his hand. He went directly up to the young girl and placed it in her hand, bending over slightly to whisper some words in her ear, intended for her alone. Later, remembering this surprising incident, the wisest among the folk of Assisi had understood that the bishop's gesture was more than an act of fatherly kindness; it was public approval of secret plans.

13

Five years had passed since the Umbrian city had been stirred by a series of singular events, the repercussions of which resounded still. Francis Bernardone, the drapery merchant's son, had publicly broken with his father, on the little ancient square in front of the cathedral. In the presence of the same Bishop Guido, to whom the young man had appealed for judgment, he had hurled a purse, jingling with coins, to the ground, stripped himself of his garments, one by one, until he stood there entirely naked, covered only by a long hairshirt. And in front of all those present he had cried out, "Henceforth I shall call Father, the only Father who is in heaven, and no longer call by this name Pietro Bernardone, my father according to the flesh."

And, to their general astonishment, the onlookers saw the bishop welcome the young rebel tenderly covering the youth's nakedness with part of his own mantle.

Since then there was no one either in the town or in the surrounding countryside who did not talk about Francis' strange adventure. Many looked upon him as a madman. When you are the son of a well-to-do merchant, when life looms so comfortably before you, what's the sense of roaming the roads dressed in the shabbiest peasant tunic, of sleeping in wattle huts, of carting lime and heavy stones in order to repair a dilapidated church—of begging one's bread like a tramp? But there were others who thought differently.

The first meeting

14   Clare, the daughter of the Offreducci, had met the one who called himself the Poverello during the long rides

on horseback which she liked so much to take. Why had she been troubled? She remembered him as the prince of the town's gay blades madly pursuing pleasure. Now he perched himself on an improvised scaffold, repairing with his own hands the façade of St. Damian, which was slowly crumbling into ruin. He roamed the town shouting, "He who will give me a stone will receive one reward from God. He who gives me two will receive two rewards from Jesus Christ!" When their eyes met, this man's look, so luminous, so beneficent, seemed to penetrate to the depths of her soul, like that look of mercy for the rich young man of whom the Gospel speaks, a look that he did not know how to obey. One of her first cousins Rufino, the silent one, the churlish one, had left all he owned to cast his lot with Francis Bernardone. What strange attraction made her, Clare, turn from her path to ride by the little friar and exchange greetings with him?

Then the day had come when, on the order of the bishop, the extraordinary religious had mounted the steps of the sanctuary and, during the High Mass in the cathedral, had addressed his fellow townsmen. Clare had been there, surrounded by her kindred. She had not forgotten a single word which she had heard. Never had she listened to a more ardent, more fervent voice. Never before had she better understood that the love of Christ is the highest truth of the Christian faith and that in all religion there is nothing that exists outside this infinite love. But is it not also true that this love, which surpasses all earthly loves, must be reciprocated? And that it asks for as much as it gives? What was she, Clare Offreduccio, giving? What could she give Christ in return?

15

The illustrations following

1. *In the winding streets of Assisi stand many houses of medieval aspect, which, with their massive wooden doors, recall the home of St. Clare and her family.*
2. *Numerous too are the fountains that murmur day and night; outlined behind the majestic lion is the silhouette of the ancient temple of Minerva.*
3. *The ruins of a powerful city-fortress dominate a calm, almost melancholy country scene.*
4. *At the left in this panorama of Assisi you may see the cathedral; at right, the basilica of St. Clare.*
5. *The chapel of the Porziuncola, fast within the basilica of St. Mary of the Angels. It was here that St. Clare and Francis of Assisi met, their encounter illumined by a blaze of torches.*
6. *A path which St. Clare must have traveled often. It leads from Assisi to St. Damian and from there to the Porziuncola.*
7. *What did the Poverello look like? We have no authentic portrait of Francis, but Cimabue, in his celebrated fresco in the basilica of Assisi, has given him the face of an ascetic.*
8. *And here is the encounter of little Clare and the young St. Francis, painted with a charming candor by an anonymous master at the turn of the thirteenth century. His painting, preserved in the church of St. Clare in Assisi, comprises eight scenes illustrating the life of Clare. Some of them are reproduced in the next group of illustrations.*

16

2.

3.

4.

5.

6.

7.

. . . like a romantic intrigue

It was all very much like a romantic intrigue. She would have liked to see Francis Bernardone, talk with him in private, and confide the torment of her soul and her hopes to him. From all appearances, everything separated them. She knew that too well. Her family belonged to the patriciate of Assisi, to that arrogant aristocracy so proud of its rights and privileges. These patricians called themselves the "majors"; for them a drapery merchant was the most contemptible of the "minors." In the violent struggle in which the hostile clans of the town faced each other in combat, supporters of the Emperor against partisans of the Pope, commoners against feudal lords, her kindred had not been on the same side as Francis. And, while she herself and her family had to seek refuge in exile in Perugia, Francis had been captured in the ranks of the enemy and had been a prisoner in Perugia, the city of the Griffon. Yet these difficulties were nothing alongside those raised by the very fact of her youth. That a young man of thirty, although he was almost a monk, or claimed to be one, should show interest in a sixteen-year-old girl would have been enough—had the fact become publicly known—to unleash the murderous fury of Clare's father and of her uncles, who could hardly be called forbearing.

But nothing could stop her now from embarking on that road to which a voice, deeper in her than reason—and well she knew it—called her. From the first Sunday of Lent when she had heard Francis speak of the only Love, her decision matured in her, and confirmed itself from Sunday to Sunday of the Lenten season. The luxury surrounding her at home began to disgust her. From

25

Rufino she was learning about a life of total renunciation in Christ, what it was like, what supernatural joys it offered. A plan was evolving. For propriety her friend Bona would accompany her, or if she could not, then her other friend Pacifica would come. Thus chaperoned she would meet the Poverello secretly so that he himself might decide the future of the girl who was entrusting herself entirely to his guidance.

And so it had been. Francis having returned to his native Assisi to preach the Advent sermons, Clare decided to seize her opportunity. The young girl and her accomplice secretly met with the young spokesman for Christ in a grove near the little church of Porziuncola which the bishop had assigned to the new religious. Immediately an astonishing dialogue took place between the two saintly souls. It was impossible to say which of the two was guiding, or preceding, the other along the paths of heaven. Is it not true that Clare inwardly had already renounced these joys of the world which the Poverello was exhorting her to abandon? And had not her heart already made the decision which he pressed on her, to give herself irrevocably to Christ? Thus the winter of 1213–1214 was spent in secret deliberations. But nothing transpired as a result of them. Slowly the child learned to become a stranger to her family which she cherished, in this palace where she had spent her childhood, in order to follow Him to whom one gives nothing if not everything.

And this is why on the night of Palm Sunday, a young girl in festive attire, flanked by two brown-clad friars holding blazing torches, arrived in front of the poor church of Porziuncola. Francis stood waiting on the threshold, the palm of his hand extended outward in welcome, a smile of brotherly affection on his face. He took Clare by the hand, led her to the altar of the Blessed Virgin, at whose feet Clare knelt reverently. "What do you seek here?" he asked her. "The mercy of the Lord and yours," replied young Clare in a firm voice. Then an improvised lyric poured forth from the saint's lips, phrases so simple and beautiful that they seemed to come not from human lips but as echoes of the mysterious joy that angels must have been feeling at that very moment.

A few hours later, in the place of the young beauty robed in satin and pearls, whom the olive trees had seen pass in shoes of the finest Florentine leather, there stood only a somber form, enveloped in a rough homespun tunic girded at the waist by a piece of rope. Clare's bare feet were sandaled, and a white linen veil covered her shorn head.

2

Clare in splendor

The portraits which preserve Clare's features allow us to
detect the secret of the unfailing energy which animated
a girl, barely eighteen, launched upon such an adventure.
It is true of the most famous of them, that of Simone
Martini in the lower basilica of Assisi, as well of the
portrait in the upper church. We do not know whether
the latter painting is the work of the Sienese master, of
his brother Donato, or of Maso. The delicate beauty of
the blond maiden which delighted eyes and stirred hearts
is still discernible in the pictures of an austere nun,
dressed in a fabric of brownish hue, her countenance
framed by the white linen veil. There is profound charm
in those attenuated almond-shaped eyes and in the re-
strained half-smile which contrasts with their almost
melancholy expression. But this oval face, this very
straight nose, this tiny mouth, closed to every vain word,
and even more this faint movement of withdrawal and
pride which the whole body seems to suggest, expresses
the unshakable stability of a soul in which determination
carries out the deepest aspirations, a soul imperturbable
in its total inner unity.

The days after the great vow

Clare was to give proof of this strength of soul on the very morrow of the holy night of the great vow. For, after having come upon her tracks and discovered her retreat, her father, her mother and her uncle descended upon the little Benedictine monastery, where Francis had hidden her, with a whole retinue of armed men. Her mother's pleas, her father's threats had no effect upon the cast-iron firmness of the decision she had just taken. Kneeling at the foot of the altar, her eyes fixed upon the crucifix, she remained stubbornly silent. And when her exasperated father and uncle made a move to seize her and drag her away by force, Clare without crying out, without struggling, made a simple gesture: she removed the veil from her head and revealed her shaven head for all to see. Actually if the nobles had known something of theology and canon law, they might have thought of objecting that the good Francis had no legitimate authority to consecrate a virgin to God and to receive her vows. But their astonishment disarmed them. They left the convent uttering futile threats, the Lady Ortolana wavering between weeping over her lost child and rejoicing as a Christian. The mysterious authority emanating from the frail young girl had conquered.

Moreover, the occurrence involved not only Clare. Soon another battle was to be waged. Clare had a younger sister Agnes. Less brilliant and stable than Clare, she may have been; the example of her older sister suddenly made her rise above herself.

30

In haste, as if to take revenge upon their older daughter,

who in their eyes was over-devout, the Offreduccio's set about to find a betrothed for their younger daughter without consulting her. There are some lights not easily hidden under a bushel. Constant surveillance, ruses and precautions of all kinds, nothing availed. On Low Monday, exactly two weeks after Clare's flight, Agnes also slipped out of the house and ran across the grove of olive trees up to the abbey of the cloistered nuns of St. Angelo where she knew that Clare had just been installed. She threw herself into her sister's arms, weeping for joy.

This time the family's reaction was frightful to behold. Boiling over with fury, the father ran once more to the monastery. He forced open the gate of the holy place, still escorted by the uncle Monaldo and his armed guards. Beaten black and blue, knocked to the ground, how could this fourteen-year-old girl defend herself? One guard was already dragging her towards the door; another held her arms; still another twisted her by the hair. Nothing less was required, vouches the chronicle, than the miraculous intervention of Him, whom everything on earth obeys, before an end could be put to this abominable scene. After collapsing on the floor at the threshold of the convent, Agnes' fragile body suddenly became so heavy, so alarmingly heavy that the angry men were forced to give up their attempt to drag the child away forcibly. And when Monaldo, insensate with fury, began to strike his niece with a mailed fist, preferring to see her dead rather than a nun, he felt a sudden pain course swiftly through his shoulder. It was so much like the Archangel's sword of fire, that he ran away screaming for mercy. Prostrate at the feet of the Master, Clare had obtained through her

31

entreaties this decisive intervention of Heaven. She had never doubted that God himself would be her ally in the battle she was waging in his name.

A new order is born

The time was propitious for these great spiritual movements. One hundred years earlier, when Bernard of Fontaines had gone to the monastery of Cîteaux, about four leagues from Dijon, all his brothers and at least twenty of their companions had decided to leave with him. The example of the young saint created a veritable contagion in the town of Assisi. Balvina was the first to catch it, then it spread to Benvenuta, whom Clare had come to know during the exile in Perugia. Then it affected Amata, the very young niece of the Offreduccio family. At the very moment of celebrating the most desirable betrothal, she renounced everything and immersed herself in the peace of the great renunciation. Then it was the turn of Fillipa, Giacoma, Illuminata, Concilia, Pacifica . . . and of so many others that such a holy litany would fill columns. The young tree, that had sprouted from the modest sprig of palm delivered one fine Sunday by Bishop Guido, now bore innumerable branches on which blossomed the multiformed flowers of a singular sanctity.

And so a new order was born, the Poor Ladies, although the young woman whom history was to regard as the foundress had not the least idea of her role. It rose alongside that order which the Poverello had as spontaneously brought into being. The Roman Council of 1215, one of the most important and decisive of the age, had ruled that henceforth no foundation of an order

32

would be authorized and that any new community would have to adopt one of the established Rules. So the young women of Assisi were first organized as Benedictine nuns. But was it possible that they could be unfaithful to the spirit of total poverty, of joyous and limitless renunciation to the Franciscan spirit, which they had received from Him who was the true guide of their souls?

As pious and as holy as the Benedictine communities meant to be, they, in keeping with the custom of the times, owned properties, often very great properties. In the cloister they were not forbidden to lead a life of certain comfort. But Clare had not escaped through the gate of the dead to seek in another dwelling the comforts she had renounced in the house of her parents. And now charged by Francis himself, she had to accept command of the young troop which had come to cluster about her. She felt responsible before God for these souls who had been entrusted to her and who had left everything behind in order to know the holy poverty which she was called upon to give to them.

This little abbess of twenty-two had no doubts about anything, certainly not about Providence. In order to do away with the usages and observances in the Benedictine tradition which did not seem to be in keeping with her true vocation, she needed nothing less than a dispensation from the Pope. So be it! She would write the Pope, she would petition him to listen to her. He did. The event confirmed the young saint's trust; everything went as she had wished. The exceptional privilege which Clare was asking of the Vicar of Christ was not like those to which the Lateran was accustomed: she asked the privilege of absolute poverty, of the daily risk cheerfully accepted, of sublime improvidence. Innocent III was the brilliant, intuitive Pope who in a glance had penetrated the heart of the Poverello when he had come humbly to expound his ideas to him. A brief, whose *incipit* he wanted to write in his own hand as a signal favor, reached the hands of the nun: "We confirm by Apostolic favor your resolution of sublime poverty and by the authority of these present letters grant that you may not be constrained by anyone to receive possessions."

The peace of St. Damian

The place in which the Abbess Clare, with gratitude and unadulterated joy, read the pontifical letter which wrested from her all the riches of this world to better prepare her for the sole possession of Eternity, still poignantly preserves for us the tangible memory of this sacrifice and this vow. It is St. Damian, the little monastery at the foot of the hill, so peaceful among the gray olive trees. Only a little oratory at the corner of a path and a row of cypress trees, standing straight like sentinels above a white wall, draw the attention of passers-by. The daughters of St. Clare no longer occupy this site, laden with the memories of their early history. They are now installed higher up on the hill, far from the basilica which preserves the body and the memory of the saint. But it is there, above all, that we must go to meditate upon Clare's example and evoke her memory.

At St. Damian everything speaks of destitution freely accepted, of renunciation in the name of the great

34   Poverello. No visitor would dream of talking above a whisper, so perceptible and present still are the virtues

that were once practiced here. There is no striving for beauty; the beauty is mysteriously tangible, proceeding neither from the forms nor works that were accomplished here, but from an indefinable deep harmony between this setting of stone and wood and the spiritual adventure which was unfolded here, realized in the soul's depth. This minuscule church, this poor choir, this dormitory in which the mere idea of our kind of comfort seems absurd and shameful—this was the austere setting in which the young girl of Assisi could best pursue her plans for total sacrifice. Francis had judged rightly in giving her St. Damian.

St. Damian . . . it was here, then, between these walls which still speak to us of her, that Clare lived her entire adult life, scarcely leaving the place in forty years.

It is in this poor oratory, situated below the low vault of the church, before this unadorned altar, near the narrow cupboard in which she kept her only treasures, some relics, that she deepened her vocation of prayer and pursued the unique experience of a soul entirely consecrated to God. It is in this little choir, in this dormitory, the sight of which shocks our sensibility, in this corner of the terrace which, it is said, she loved, where she must have conducted the silent colloquy that no human lips can ever translate. One must meditate long in this place, and let oneself be penetrated by the supernatural peace that emanates from it to understand entirely how happiness can be born of the fullness of sacrifice. It is the proper setting for prayers that surge forth from souls in renunciation, a setting austere, inhuman, which disturbs our sensibilities but where, nonetheless, our souls mysteriously feel at peace.

In the presence of this spectacle which the little monastery offers us, the Franciscan ideal as it was conceived by Clare of Assisi and her sisters impresses itself upon the mind with such force of evidence that one must have lost all sense of spiritual things and be completely uprooted from the Christian faith not to feel and understand its lessons. The awesome words of Christ, on which we do not dare meditate and which torment us, we see embodied and acquiesced to here.

Those women would have renounced everything then, given all their possessions to the poor, and taken up their cross in order to follow Him. Those women, embarked upon the arduous path of heaven, like the apostles earlier had set out on the roads of the world, must have carried neither money, nor reserves, nor cloaks, nor staffs. Self-deprivation pushed to such an extreme clashes so violently with our nature that something wicked in each of us would want to belie these women and the lesson which they propose. But then all the misery of the world comes to their rescue, all the abjectness and perishability that we see around us. It is the taste of ashes on our lips that makes us feel the supernatural peace which reigns at Saint Damian as water of an exquisite freshness.

Do not think for a moment that the asceticism which Clare dictated ever became inhuman or risked compromising the very plan it proposed. There is nothing more touching in the chronicles which tell us of her life than the little recorded incidents which show the saint maternally eager to aid her daughters and to give them all earthly help compatible with the Rule and with their own needs. If for herself she took no account and demanded of her own body more than it could legitimately give, she was very careful to limit reasonably the zeal of others.

True, her community was exemplary for the silence observed, for the piety that marked it, for the fasts and abstinences it practiced. But in winter, when it was cold, the abbess herself would rise and make certain that all the sisters were well covered. If one of them were sick, a special nourishment was prepared for her, a mattress was placed on her plank. And, if any of the sisters appeared tormented, afflicted, there was no tenderness and affectionate attention that Clare did not give in order to restore peace of heart to her. A beautiful anecdote tells of the saint personally welcoming those of her daughters who had consecrated themselves to begging in the streets for the bread of the community, she herself removing their sandals, washing their tired feet and kissing them as Magdalene kissed those of Jesus . . .

Forty years of work and prayer

For nearly forty years such was the life of Clare of Assisi at the little monastery of St. Damian. The noises of the world died out on the threshold of the little square upon which the portal of their church opened. Only some events which concerned the two Orders of the Poor really interested her. Whole communities of other congregations beseeched the Poor Ladies to accept them as members. Beloved Francis, their admirable guide, had gone far away, very far, as far as the Orient it was said, to bring the message of truth to the Sultan of Egypt and to pray at the Holy Sepulchre. The happiest news came from Morocco: five friars, sent by their order to bear their witness, had the honor of shedding their blood for the divine Master, martyred by Miramolin. These supernatural joys were the only ones that could enter into these cloistered

37

souls in whom contemplation left no further room for
that which troubles men's hearts and agitates their minds.

These forty years were spent in this face-to-face encounter with the one and only God. The repeated, inexhaustible prayer, to which Clare abandoned herself for
long hours every day, was in effect the more precise
formulation of an incessant prayer which filled her days
to the brim from her early rising until night and which
consecrated the least of her actions. In this permanent
communion with Christ is it surprising that many a time
the supernatural should burgeon in her like spring water
in an undergrowth? Chroniclers report that one day there
was no oil at all in the monastery, but a simple word of
the saint sufficed to fill up jars—to the utter amazement
of the mendicant Franciscan friar who had just arrived
with some. And then a leper, sent by St. Francis to St.
Damian, having hoisted himself as best he could on the
ladder which led to the monastery's only entrance, later
descended it with the adroitness of an athlete, totally
healed by one word murmured by the saint. Equally
famous is the episode of the assault launched against the
pious dwelling by a band of Saracens whom the impious
Emperor Frederick had unleashed over Italy. They ran off
in panic at the mere sight of the saint standing at the door
of the convent refectory, beautiful with a terrible calm,
holding the ciborium containing the Blessed Sacrament.
But all of this, all these incidents, large and small, of a
golden legend borrowed from history are valuable only
as signs. Clare lived in Christ. Christ was present in her.
There was no need for miracles and spectacular events for
this union to exist.

38

The *"little plant" of St. Francis*

Such was the destiny of this young girl, whose very name signifies radiance and splendor, in the light of Assisi at a crucial hour when the Umbrian city was a beacon lighting the Christian world. Taking up an expression which one day had been uttered with such tenderness by the founder, she liked to call herself "the little plant of our father Francis." We must not be misled by this humility. The plant, in its species, was just as great and as admirable as that of the brown-clad friars. And at the same time it was multiplying its own cuttings. The Order of the Poor Ladies must not be seen in the shadow of the masculine Order; the daughters of St. Clare also bore an important witness, alongside the sons of the Poverello. Indeed, in the deepest sense of the term they perfected the witness of their brethren.

It goes without saying that the work accomplished by Clare can only be understood in terms of a plan completely outside that of material efficacies, and it can be appreciated only by one who knows the supernatural power of contemplation. The fact that human beings—

39

men or women—be they Clares or Carmelites, Cistercians or Carthusians, although they do not leave their convents and do nothing but raise up an invisible monument of prayers to heaven, are, in truth, intense activists may seem absurd and derisible to those who measure the results of human activity according to the canons of power or money. But for those who, once and for all, have understood that a dependent link and a total causality exist between the invisible and the visible, for those who know that our acts on earth are but a reflection of the supreme ordinance of heaven, the work of the cloisters appears in its true form, bathed in its own light. Maybe they determine the course of things to a far greater degree than we know.

Alongside the ardent friarly cohort whom the thirteenth century watched bravely set out upon the roads of the world to teach the gospel anew, were those equally fervent but retiring troops, silent, motionless, whose battlefields were a dilapidated choir, a miserable dormitory, a refectory pledged to bread and water. But their ceaseless, impassioned assistance was showered on the journeying preacher, on the missionary risking his life among the infidels, on the whole order engaged in its harsh battles. Francis had understood all this when he accepted his sister Clare in that place where we have seen her, at his side.

A supernatural friendship

40   The deep harmony, at once so complete and unequivocal, which from the beginning had existed between Francis Bernardone and Clare Offreduccio, lasted through-

out their lives, though each of them had to assume re-
sponsibilities as head of an Order and be absorbed in its
labors. The indefinable tenderness in the Poverello's sensibility suggested the gentle presence of a woman. At the
feet of her whom he called his Lady, he was like the
troubador of the courts of love. But his love was addressed
only to the Lady without stain, to Mary, pure and im-
maculate. The formidable virtue of renunciation which
others might envision as a peevish old crone in tatters,
was for him a vigorous and gracious virgin whom he
called "Lady Poverty." Everything he loved, everything
he sang as the great poet he was, naturally assumed
feminine terms: water "humble and chaste" was his
sister, and "Mother Earth," just as death, on the day of his
supreme inspiration, was to be his last friend.

It is Clare, the luminous image, that adds so much to
the portrait of Francis, Clare who invests with a visible
presence the femininity he loved. This does not mean that
there was a great intimacy between them, nor that their
encounters were frequent. The founder always exhibited
a tactful and discrete reserve towards her whom he had
led to God; he wanted her destiny to unfold in total
freedom and her responsibility to be complete. Francis
took care not to interfere overmuch in matters affecting the
Order of the Poor Ladies, even when they themselves
would have wished to see him concern himself more with
them. He spoke firmly only to moderate the excessive
ardor of his younger sister in her self-mortification. According to the chronicles, it was Francis who compelled
her to give up the vine branches on which she slept and
replace them with a straw mat. Such acts define the
exquisite delicacy of their friendship before God.

41

The friars hatch a pleasant plot

The discretion that marked Francis' behavior towards the nuns of St. Damian was so great that his own friars, undoubtedly aware of their complaints, let him know that his aloofness astonished the sisters. A pleasant plot was hatched which turned out to be a remarkable success. Goaded by his companions, the Poverello agreed to share a repast with his friend "in order to discourse together about the love of Christ." On the appointed day, accompanied by her dear Pacifica, Clare went to St. Mary of the Angels: she had prepared for this colloquy by devoting the whole morning to prayers. Ten years later, within her still and intact, was the emotion which she had felt on that cool night of Palm Sunday when she had escaped from the parental home to find this guide to whom the Lord was entrusting her. The meeting took place; the repast began. Be assured that it was a meal of perfect frugality, even served on the ground, the grass for a tablecloth and stumps of trees for chairs. The friars who had somehow prepared everything for them doubtlessly were looking forward to a profusion of human joys, to one of those happy moments of relaxation when it is permitted, while praising the Creator, to take a little pleasure in the good things he has created. But this sublime repast unfolded in an atmosphere quite different from that of a little country feast.

For, hardly were they seated by each other, when both saints felt such a fullness of love for Him who had permitted all these things, and such certainty that this collation was but a sign and the pledge of the celestial repast promised to the elect, that their voices rose in the silence,

42

responding to each other in lauds and invocations. A hymn of gratitude, one of the most beautiful that he had ever composed, poured forth from the lips of the poet. He expressed his happiness in belonging to the one and only Master, in having renounced all the affections of this world. He trumpeted the praise of holy Poverty to whom all these men and women had given themselves. He glorified the splendor of this unique day, the sweetness and the beauty of the world, which are the tangible reflection of an ineffable love.

The chronicler tells us that this most singular repast was suddenly interrupted by the whirlwind arrival of neighboring peasants, townsfolk and passers-by. All of them had seen an unusual light rise above the woods where this mystic dialogue was in progress. They had thought it was a fire, but no, it was the flaming souls of Francis and Clare which had brilliantly illumined the whole countryside.

Only death was to put an end to this supernatural friendship, so moderate in human expression and so unrestrained in Godly praise. Worn out prematurely by a life of struggles and privations, Francis was now but a skinny, pale form. Only the soul maintained life in the exhausted body and held its mortal case. The journey to the Orient had finished undermining his health. Was it necessary that at this very moment his conscience be wrecked by torments born of the evolution of his Order, which forced upon him the painful realization that the sublime anarchy of Porziuncola and of Rivo Torto was no longer enough?

In appearance, everything was going splendidly with the Order. Its rapid growth went far beyond its founder's

43

hopes. One after the other, the popes showed a very special benevolence to the friars. But a deep anxiety tore at Francis' heart. He asked himself whether the work which he had brought into being would continue to develop according to the intentions of Providence, whether the new tendencies he discerned in its ranks were not synonyms for infidelity. And when Clare came to tell him that he should speak more firmly and more solemnly proclaim the ideal which had given its name to their life, he replied with the most gentle smile that he did not have to solicit the designs of holy Providence, that he wanted to be a living sign, a simple witness, not a chief who issued commands. Had not the Lord himself done thus in refusing to use his power and accepting his delivery to his enemies?

It was to this total trust that Christ in person responded. He ordained that through suffering and death Francis would be the living sign that he wished to be.

The death of St. Francis

Utterly exhausted, tortured by the wounds that no medicine could close, half-blind, the Poverello petitioned the Master on the high mountain of Alverno, where he had come to meet him in solitude, to bring his own suffering to a height that he might fully share in those of the Cross. It was then, in an hour of ecstasy, when the fifth ray struck his body, that Francis—the perfect imitator of Christ—received the stigmata of the holy wounds in his hands, his feet, his side. For him, thenceforth, all earthly things had been accomplished.

44 All that remained for Francis was the slow, meticulous, mystic approach of death. Never had Clare, whose heart of flesh was torn asunder to see the signs pointing to this approach, felt more closely united with her guide, more closely linked with his willingness to sacrifice. A supernatural joy emanated from this dying man, momentarily reprieved, with the great lyric transports of his most beautiful poems, the "Canticle to Brother Sun," and the "Canticle of Creatures." At St. Damian, where he had asked to be carried in memory of his youth, Clare's devotion had taxed all its energies and resources to nurse his wounds, which the compresses of aromatic herbs she lovingly applied to them failed to heal. But more important than her ministrations to the body during the last halt before death's approach, had been once again the colloquy of souls, this certainty by which each reassured the other that both had successfully walked along the paths the Lord had commanded them to follow.

When Brother Francis felt the hour of the Angel approach, one of his last thoughts was for his dear sister cloistered in St. Damian. A friar, bearer of the last message that Francis had the strength to dictate, was dispatched to the small convent. The saint ordered Clare to banish all grief. He also promised her that at the hour of her death she would again see him whom she had regarded as her older brother, as her guide, and that he would guard over her from the fold of the Father, never forsaking her. Giotto has evoked the last image of this supra-terrestrial friendship, which history has preserved for us. It portrays Clare bent over the body of her friend, her face strained with supernatural attentiveness. In this face-to-face encounter she seems to be receiving a supreme lesson in peace and love from him.

45

Clare's work continues

What is there to say about the life of St. Clare after the death of St. Francis? It was on October 3, 1226 that the Master summoned Francis' soul to him; twenty-seven years were to pass before his friend was to hearken to the same summons. More than ever now, this nun's existence was isolated from the world. She was a voluntary prisoner of her own disciplines, entirely absorbed in contemplation. Even the purest joys that she could know, in some way remained external to her being: the arrivals at the convent first of her sister Beatrice, then of her mother, Ortolana, whom the death of her husband finally permitted to obey a long-heard secret summons; the prodigious growth of the Order of the Poor Ladies everywhere, not only in Italy, but in France, in Spain, in Austria, and even in Bohemia. All this was consequence, result: she knew the origin of the force that had ordered all this into being.

It was not long before illness assailed this body. The excessive fastings and the rigors of asceticism had prepared it only too well. Over and over again, her community expected to see illness triumph over the resistance of this unconquered soul which a weak body ceaselessly betrayed. But no, the task which Clare had to fulfill on earth was not yet finished. She had to resist, as had Francis, the all-too-human tendencies which threatened to make her Order turn aside from its original concept. She had obtained from their old friend, Cardinal Hugolino, now Pope Gregory IX, the express confirmation of that privilege of poverty which was the true pride of their observances. In this sense Clare was more fortunate than Francis. She was to be given that most beautiful of

46

rewards, the joy of hearing the sanctity of her friend pronounced before the whole Church. She herself was fully aware of the mysterious connection between two actualities: it was Francis from the height of heaven who had obtained the privilege for the daughters of Clare to be Poor Ladies until the end of time.

In the face of death that was gliding towards her with an irresistible, muffled tread, Clare remained as always a tempered blade of steel, under the aspect of an exquisite sweetness. To a cardinal who had come to visit her, and who had found her very ill, she replied with these simple words to which her whole life bequeathed authority: "No suffering has ever troubled me, no penance has ever burdened me, no sickness has ever been too arduous." And this was true.

The amazing energy which distinguished her character never left her, even at the end. Nor did her infinite charity, this need to give herself to others, to sacrifice herself. It was during the humble performance of one of these customary chores, closing the big front door of the monastery—from which as abbess she could have been exempt—that the accident occurred which was finally to break her physical strength. Knocked to the ground by the heavy fantail of the door which had been torn from its hinges, bleeding, injured internally, but still calm and smiling, she put up a bare resistance to the hurt that was destroying her. More than ever now, having cast off from the earth's mooring, she put to sea for the great voyage of the soul. Every day she recited the office of the Passion that had been composed by the Poverello, united by her sufferings, her fevers, by her waiting to Him who had become a Man of Sorrows to redeem all mankind.

47

The death of St. Clare

Then came the last response. One evening, in the little choir of St. Damian, while the saint, feverish, utterly exhausted, was meditating upon the same Christ, who a long time before had spoken to Francis, she felt herself being penetrated through by the pain of the Crucified. So totally did she share, that she ceased to belong to the earth and, still living, actually entered into heaven. Feeling herself grow faint, she made her way back to her cell. Even so her ecstasy did not come to an end. She remained thus for hour upon hour, rigid, her eyes fixed straight in front of her on some indefinable but invisible and wondrous vision. The nuns who came to watch over her by turn knew the meaning of this strange state. Their father Francis was about to keep the promise that he had made to his friend: he was coming to receive her soul into the court of heaven.

On August 12, 1253 a procession, at once sorrowful, joyful and triumphant, carried the body of the perfect saint of the Master. It wended from St. Damian towards the church of St. George along the mountainous, stony, difficult path which pilgrims still piously tread. Pope Innocent IV and cardinals in goodly number, and all the brown-clad friars who had been able to rush to the spot joined the silent troop of Poor Ladies. Clare, the little plant, was returning to the faithful earth in which she would take root so that great harvests would spring. And the light of a beautiful day in Assisi seemed to be the visible reflection of her splendor.

Contemplation: Clare's Inner Splendor ═══

4

The witness of Clare

Like the flame that rose from the lamps of the wise
virgins, Clare's inner splendor shines loftily and purely in
the majestic Franciscan edifice, next to the light of the
Poverello which does not dim it. These figures, who
sprang from Christian fervor at its most ardent pitch, add
two new dimensions to the countenance of lived sanctity.
Their witness does not resemble those of many great souls
before them or those which lofty mystics after them were
to mark with their own distinctive characters. This pro-
liferation of sanctity, its permanent renewal, the multi-
plicity of the forms in which it expresses and manifests in
history the fire of the only Love, is a fact that never ceases
to amaze us. But what is even more amazing, more admirable, is that these two had risen side by side, in the
same place, in the same time, each bound to the other by
the most tenacious roots, closely associated in their wills,
and supernaturally complementary to each other.

Who is Francis of Assisi? In the eyes of the world, a
man of action, even if his methods appear unusual and
paradoxical, even if they were nearly always opposite of
the means practiced by the apologetics of his time. True,

we know we must understand the whole activity of God's sublime adventurer in relation to the supernatural realities from which his indefatigable energy drew its nourishment in silence and meditation. But it is no less true that the Poverello, observed from without, is a man always on the road, roaming the provinces of Italy and the countries of the world, a man who harangues crowds, who presides over assemblies, who pleads the cause of his undertaking in Rome, who dreams of an Africa that must be evangelized, and who, as the first of the new kind of missionary, at great personal risk, brings the Truth under the very tents of Islam. Appearing at a time when the conscience of Christendom was confronted with new and arduous problems, when the baptized dough, once more ready to fall, needed to be stirred anew so that the leaven of the Lord might act upon it, when the continuing violence of the centuries added new fuel to the injustices of King Money, Francis, the frail little man of Assisi, seemed surely, providentially, the one to assume the responsibility of seizing with both hands the tasks that were imposed upon the Church, and of bearing public witness to the sweetness and renunciation that Christ teaches, by word and deed.

The fruits of contemplation

In all appearances Clare's witness to Christ is of an entirely different character. The mystic sister of Francis bore her witness in the innermost recesses of the most humble of cloisters. Never, throughout her life, would anyone see her proclaim to others the great certitudes that gave meaning to her life. Upon learning of the martyrdom of the Franciscans in Morocco, she had thought of becoming a missionary, but this had been only a plan: it was not her true destiny to roam the roads of distant lands. In some forty years she was never to walk along a road longer than that which rises from St. Damian to Assisi, or that which, starting out from the humble monastery, winds its way through the olive trees and the vineyards and leads to Porziuncola.

Her very renunciation, the privilege of total poverty that she had received from the Pope as a grace, had not the characteristics of Francis'. For him, poverty, besides the powerful supernatural virtues which he undoubtedly recognized in it, was a kind of an apologetics by example. In the face of a world haunted by the growing temptation of money, the little brown-clad friars who begged for their food, raised a protest, a protest anyone could comprehend by looking at their way of life. Clare's renunciation, and that of her sisters, was totally private, concealed between the walls of their monastery. Their vow of renunciation was carried out and assumed significance under the eyes of God alone. If both Francis and Clare made an essential contribution to Christian life, they certainly did not do so by the same methods. The nun had supported the Church as fully as her brother before God, and she deserved to be portrayed at his side in Giotto's famous fresco which depicts the Poverello holding up the crumbling pillars of the temple. In this singular work each saint helped in his own way.

Why, then, did Francis, by God's will the trusted guide of this predestined soul, choose to direct her along this path of pure mysticism? Why did he let her create the

53

kind of a cloistered convent in which collective poverty, humble and daily labor, regulated prayer throughout the day, seemed to serve only the personal edification of those who practiced this discipline, and who did not seem to be obliged to be active in a world in need of such lessons. For Clare and her daughters, poverty was an ineffable joy with which, according to her own expression, she "had made a very sweet pact." It was a way of understanding contempt for the goods of this world more shattering than that of Francis, who compared money to the grimiest dust, and who once ordered one of his monks to eat donkey dung to atone for the fault of accepting money.

It is here that we touch upon the deepest mystery of the Christian soul, upon the secret springs from which flow the living waters within our being. Such is the absolute principle: in order to be effective in the world, one who bears witness to Christ must be more than enterprising, courageous, able and energetic, these are but human qualities. St. Paul had said it, and St. Francis was to repeat it over and over again. However, he must above all nourish himself on the intangibles which consecrate these qualities and order them to their purpose. Temporal effort is nothing if it is not supported, guided and illumined by prayer: contemplation alone nourishes action.

Thus did Clare's work, the silent task of the second order, add to and co-operate with the vast labors accomplished by Francis and his missionaries of God. This second order, as Father Gemelli has admirably expressed it, "is the most beautiful achievement of the interior apostolate, just as St. Clare personifies to the highest degree the Franciscan ideal of prayer, piety and of joy." While their brothers vigorously kneaded the human dough, which

54

was then so resistant, the Poor Clares elected supernatural paths. We must clearly understand at which point these two parallel efforts join and while admiring their achievements, know how to distinguish them.

Clare, counselor to Francis

It is not too much to say that Francis loved, admired, and venerated her whom he delighted to call "brighter than light." And that very often, in hours of trial and perhaps anguish which saints escape no more than other mortals, his thoughts must have turned in the direction of this little monastery from which a most pure, totally disinterested, and endless prayer rose towards the Byzantine crucifix which had made him hear the voice of the Master. He regarded her as indispensable and, according to the plans of Providence, she most certainly was.

In the days of her adolescence when she had left the parental roof to join Francis from who she expected everything, Clare had been his pupil. But very soon the situation was reversed. The soul of the young abbess was so evidently full of God, so illumined by wisdom, that the head of all the Franciscans often asked advice from the humble nun of St. Damian. There is no doubt that the great decisions concerning the Order were made in agreement with Clare. We know that she was the "peaceful source" of the "Canticle to Brother Sun." We also know that she received the confidences of the seraphic Father when he was tormented by changes in the spirit of Franciscanism. Clare's role of counselor was so well established that Pope Gregory IX made her his confidante,   *55* and after the death of Francis those of his brothers who

The illustrations following

9. *A scene from the life of St. Clare (detail from a painting in the basilica of St. Clare, Assisi). Bishop Guido gives Clare a blessed palm.*

10. *Clare receives her habit. St. Francis is about to cut her hair.*

11. *A crucial scene: Clare's parents have come to the convent to find their daughter and vainly try to take her away by force.*

12. *Clare's "daughters" are installed in the large convent beside the basilica where the body of the saint is now venerated.*

13. *St. Damian, the miserable ruin where the abbess Clare is cloistered for the rest of her life.*

14. *There is not always enough to eat in the refectory of the Poor Ladies, but the holy abbess never doubts in God's providence.*

15. *Through the frame of the choir door in the convent of St. Damian, we see a stairway leading to the dormitory.*

16. *The dying saint is blessed with a celestial vision: the Virgin escorted by angels appears to her.*

56

13.

14.   15.

16.

wanted to remain as faithful as possible to his message
could not think of a better guarantor than the person who
had first received it.

There were times when Clare's counsel determined that
of Francis. This was especially true at the beginning of
their common work. The Poverello, who had let himself
be so well guided by his inner voice when it was a question of breaking with his family, his life, the world, could
no longer exactly discern the route to follow. Should he
like the hermits of the desert shut himself away in some
solitary place to pray there in total renunciation to the
one and only God. Or should he go and proclaim the
Word in public squares and strets among the throngs who
failed to recognize it? Francis had charged Clare to decide the issue. Greatly moved to guide her guide in this
way, after having prayed long to the Holy Spirit and
meditated at length during nights of vigil, she replied.
According to the chronicle, Francis received the messenger, who transmitted the reply to him, on his knees,
his arms crossed, as if the Lord himself, through the voice
of a little nun of twenty-three or twenty-four, had hurled
his supreme order at him, "Go ye and teach all nations."

Later, very much later, when a crisis threatened the
existence of the Order, when Francis suffered at the sight
of certain of his friars deviating from the only path he
thought capable of leading his work to its conclusion, it
was to Clare still that he went to disclose his fears and his
decisions. It was to her that he confided that he had first
thought of restoring the rebels to obedience by showing
them "what kind of a will his was." But thinking of Him
who had wanted to conquer the world only through his
defeat and whose greatest claim of triumph was the Cross,
Francis renounced his intention. He had come to ask

65

Clare to confirm him in this resolution, to speak to him one more time in the name of the Great Defeated One, the Great Loser of the earth. He would not join battle; instead, he would climb to the top of the high mountain of Alverno there to wait for a reply to his questions, if it so pleased the Lord. Above all, he asked spiritual assistance from Clare.

And this is essential. If Francis turned to the nun of St. Damian for assistance in making his most difficult choices, it was not only because he knew her to be wise, prudent, well informed, luminously intelligent; he recognized all these qualities in her, but were they the main reason for his recourse to her? What Francis, the leading activist, awaited from the cloistered nun, was something else: the supernatural power of prayer. He, who had lived totally in God, knew better than any person that nothing which comes to pass here below, none of the actions which men seem freely to decide, has any meaning except an imperceptible design of which only the prayer of saints can break the continuity. Just as Moses, according to Scripture, had prayed on the hilltop while his troops fought the enemy in the plain, so did the Franciscan army enlist the sovereign efficacious aid of those who serve through prayer in the rough battles which it had to fight. Clare's contemplation, and that of her sisters, rightly appears as one of the determining elements in the great Franciscan achievement. And who can say whether the Order of the Friars Minor would have achieved the prodigious success that it did, and have grown, with the joyous alacrity that we have seen, into tens and soon into hundreds of holy houses, had not women, dedicated to God, in accordance with the same spirit moved Providence in the very depths of the mystery of his designs, and obtained his support.

5

At St. Damian

If one wants to penetrate the secret of St. Clare it is to St. Damian that one must go, to this little monastery at the foot of the Assisian hill which has changed so little in the past seven hundred years. Everything there still speaks of her: all is harmony with the memory of her virtues and her deeds. The landscape has remained about the same as when her sandals turned over the stones strewn along the rough path. A lone olive tree still seems to mount a guard of prayer. And the cypresses, behind the holy cloister, visibly defy men and time.

Holy poverty is perceptible here, present everywhere. The modest façade—which Clare did not know—had kept the barnlike appearance it must have had in her time, a celestial barn where the harvests of concealed virtues are piled up. The church, the minute *chiesina,* lower than the ground, is no richer now than during the days when the first Clares came to relieve their holy guide at the foot of that large Byzantine crucifix which with a look miraculously had snatched him from himself, and let the inner call of God resound in his soul. The choir of the nuns, above all, makes a striking impression of absolute renunciation, of willed poverty. These rough-hewn desks, these benches which do not even have elbow-rests, these irregular slabs visibly worn down by the generation of kneeling—was this truly the setting in which these girls could have had joy in living? They were for the most part members of the well-to-do nobility, who had been raised in comfort and riches and whom nothing had habituated to austerities of this kind. One can vividly imagine them, stretched out side by side on the hard planks or on the rough straw sacks in the dormitory of the Poor Ladies, with its crudely cast walls and its poorly squared exposed beams, resting as they waited for the nocturnal reveille, a funeral call or so we imagine it: the memory troubles our tender hearts.

Yet what is this mysterious joy that invades the soul and permeates it everywhere in these places which bear the inscription of sacrifice? In the church, in the choir, in this narrow space which is called the "little sepulchre," the *sepulcreto,* where the bodies of the first Clares are only a memory mixed with the earth, even in this dormitory with its grim austerity, there reigns a peace which does not come from the joys of the world. It affects even the most inattentive visitor. And more than anywhere else, this mysterious happiness is perceptible, and penetrates the heart on the narrow terrace (one enters by a low door) where Clare customarily sat. This terrace is so tiny that one might call it a niche, indeed one must bend in order to pass through. It is here that the memory of the saint becomes a tangible presence. Here, all is purity, calm, all is meditation and silence; two cypresses, their boughs gently, almost imperceptibly, quivering, stand guard over the terrace, a corner of which is brightened by geraniums. In the distance, to the west, the blue and pink Appennines seem to rarify matter. They are only a form, a dream. Everything must have been just like this when Clare sat here to prolong her prayer. And the secret charm of this miniature landscape seems to exist in order to recall, to those who forget it, the fervent soul's mysterious power, to link the beauty of things to its ineffable origin when all creation is illumined by the interior fire of contemplation.

Contemplation: secret source of joy

Contemplation: this is the key word, the one which summarizes and characterizes Clare's activity, her long days, which were always the same, and her entire existence in the eyes of God. In his story of her life and miracles the good Thomas of Celano says simply: "Her soul ceaselessly gave itself up to prayer." The first to rise, as was her habit, she would go to awaken the younger among the sisters without breaking the silence, inspiring them by her countenance to begin the day in fervor. Then all through the day, never remaining idle, she prayed without cease, regardless of the task in which she was engaged. There is no better definition of the nature of St. Clare's contemplative experience—which indeed is the very essence of contemplation—than by rereading these wholly simple lines so evidently truthful.

For a heaven-oriented soul like Clare's, contemplation was not an extraordinary activity, to be added to the varied chores of life, nor did it require show or preparation of any kind. No, the spirit of prayer, the meditation in God, naturally joined with the daily, the humdrum, the humble reality of the familiar, the indispensable tasks.

69

One cannot understand the phenomenon of contemplation without this wondrous simplicity.

For her, to contemplate—and this word that belongs to
the language of spirituality was not in her vocabulary—
was to live in the presence of God, nothing more, nothing
less. As the last sentence of the blessing which she left to
her sisters says: "May the Lord be with you at all times!
And may you be always in Him!"

In a paragraph of her Rule, we read this counsel:
"While working, never let the spirit of prayer and devotion be extinguished, which all other temporal things
must serve." Thus contemplation is not something external to the activities of life. On the contrary, it is constantly associated with them; ultimately, it is contemplation that endows them with their true significance.

In a sense one can say that contrary to what frivolous
people may think, it almost disappears and is absorbed in
daily realities. The flame of prayer did not burn any
higher in St. Clare's soul when she prostrated herself
before the choir than when she was working with her
hands, or teaching her daughters, or amusing herself with
them in recreation. But, in another sense, it is evident
that the intention must be supreme and that it is supreme.
It covers an unlimited field, because prayer is continuous,
indefinite, associated with all activities of life. And the
height to which it can reach is limitless as well because
it is the spirit of prayer which gives meaning to the most
banal tasks, to the most menial of earthly chores by as-
sociating the whole of one's being with God even in the
servitude of earthly destiny and the misery of the human
condition.

70

But is it even a question of "association?" Actually it

is something more, an intimate fusion. The phrase "adhere to God" which the French mystics of the *grand siècle* were so fond of using is one all contemplatives must reckon with. Contemplation, and this certainly was the way St. Clare understood it, is nothing else but the effort, continuing or concluded, to unite man totally with God. All in human nature must be ordered to this goal: the mind must apply itself to know the things of God. St. Paul sought only this; he already defined this fourfold requirement when he made his celebrated avowal: "And I live, now not I, but Christ liveth in me." To succeed in interiorizing God to the point of becoming one with him, in the reality of his presence, is the consummation of the act of contemplation.

The way of perfection

It would be easy to show that St. Clare's spirit of prayer never deviated from these simple and precise definitions. But it would be excessive and inexact to speak of the "spirit of St. Clare," as though her contemplation revealed an originality that separated it from others, from the spirit of the Benedictine nuns, say, or from those of Carmel. In its plenitude the mystic impulse defies classification and category. The spirit of the great spiritualists does not wish to be named: it is only the spirit of Christ, but a spirit which is lived, tested, and realized in all its demands. A brief sentence in the Rule of St. Clare, the one which tells her sisters that the ideal to which they must dedicate themselves is simply "to live according to the perfection of the holy Gospel," is a reminder that she never lost sight of this profound truth.

When we try to penetrate the secrets of this soul we cannot help but discern differences, and dwell unduly on what is but a minor variant. We have seen that the most extreme form of renunciation was the point of departure for her spiritual itinerary; the Franciscan way is that of poverty, and not only a poverty recognized as something useful in practice, but poverty which is a virtue in itself, which strips the soul and frees it from its shackles. This renunciation is not a mutilation, because the goods one sacrifices, material, intellectual, and even spiritual are found again in God.

In the same way as renunciation, another benefit evolves from this experience: simplicity. In her last testament St. Clare invites her sisters never to stray from its oath. Perhaps, its other name is the childlike spirit to whose possessors the Kingdom was promised. There is to be no spectacular attitude of any kind, no excessive outward show: spiritual colloquy is carried on in freedom and in the holy familiarity of a happy love. This is how St. Clare, like her guide and friend St. Francis, understood it. Truth has no patience with certain airs, and intelligence finds little worth in certain words. All is pure, all is simple; there is no trumpeting or exhibitionism in the Franciscan perspective. Meditation, prayer, contemplation are so natural that they become like the air one breathes. One hardly knows they are there and that one takes life from them.

There remains only a question of methods. There is a unique quality about the very plan that the contemplative soul follows, even so the individual features of it may vary. The great truths of Franciscan spirituality are manifested in Clare's soul at prayer. First of all, the predominant love of God become man, of the living Jesus, teaching and dying.

We know about lofty mystics who, according to the times, according to temperament, sought "adhesion" to God in others ways: by contemplating the mystery of the Holy Trinity, by placing themselves in the light of the Third Person, by adoring the God present in the sacrament of the altar, and by still others means. For Clare, as for St. Francis and the whole Franciscan tradition, it is Jesus, the Son of God, the Son of Man who truly, according to the word, is the Way, the Truth, the Life.

In the twelfth century St. Bernard had been most instrumental in the discovery of the human, fraternal Christ, wondrously close to our anxieties and hopes. And in his time nobody more than the Poverello of Assisi had spread and communicated this discovery, perfecting it in a thousand ways. It was also through St. Francis that Clare learned to praise the Lord. She meditated constantly upon the at once human and superhuman destiny of Jesus. Innumerable are the texts in which her pen gives expression to this preoccupation, which truly excluded any other: "Jesus is the splendor of glory, the light of the eternal light, the mirror without tarnish. Look all through the day into this mirror, and contemplate your visage therein. It is there that you will see in festive array the most numerous and varied virtues, like a profusion of flowers."

The objects of meditation

Each act of the drama which was the life of the Lord was the object of her meditation: the Infant in the Crib whose humility was an example to her, the Teacher of

73

Truth whose word will never pass away and above all, the Man of Sorrows whose suffering takes upon itself and redeems all the sufferings of the earth, and for whom the contemplative nun nourished an inexhaustible compassion: "Meditate constantly," she told her sister Ermentrude, upon the mysteries of the Cross and upon the sorrows of his mother who stood at the foot of the Cross."

Clare wanted nothing else but to live with her eyes fixed upon the only Model, to imitate in her life the least of his acts, to practice the least of his monitions. Did not she, who gave this supreme counsel in a letter to Agnes of Bohemia, "By dint of contemplating God transform your whole self into the image of God," put into practice what two centuries later another mystic was to call "the imitation of Christ"?

However, this absorbing love of God become man, which in the following century was to be emphasized with an emotion that was often overwhelming, knew in the time of Clare and Francis how to preserve a characteristic note of sweetness and serenity in singing the praises of God. The oblation which the contemplative individual makes of himself and of his soul is a peaceful one. It is first of all an act of thanksgiving. Through all his being he participates in the world around him, in this marvelous world of the creation which the Poverello was the first to discover, whose splendors he glorified in song better than anyone. This is why Franciscan mysticism is the most deeply human and why it stirs us to our depths. A stream of poetry runs through it which embraces and gathers towards God all living things, everything which surrounds man: beasts as well as plants, the sun, crystalline water, the wind, in order to consecrate them to him. The

great discovery of Franciscanism was that the sinful earth
is also the splendid work of the Creator on which the
mark of his glory is visibly inscribed. Clare, too, made
this discovery—Clare who loved trees, flowers, landscapes,
animals (in her biographies there is a charming story of
a little cat participating in a miracle) and who, as her
mortal life drew to its close, knew so well how to recognize joy.

Joy: an attitude

Joy! This is the conclusive word for Franciscan spirituality and the methods of contemplation that Clare
taught her daughters. Or was it teaching? Even more, it
was an attitude towards life, one so natural and instinctive
that the least gesture bore witness to this joy. It inex-
haustibly and spontaneously poured forth in the least
word: "It even seemed," writes Thomas of Celano, "that
bodily suffering made divine love and interior joy grow
in her. Despite her penances, she preserved a joyous
countenance, as though nothing caused her to suffer or as
though Grace allowed her to hold all corporal afflictions
in disdain. Indeed the sufferings of the flesh made her
rejoice, because they alleviated the weariness of the heart."
And even the cruelest torments of the soul, those which
a Christian suffers to the point of anguish and sorrow
when he thinks about the sinfulness of the world, and of
his own complicities therein, and about the appalling
tragedy which was its consequence and conclusion, the
Passion, did not impair the supernatural joy welling over
in the heart of the saint. For the contemplative soul, sufferings accepted and willed for the sake of the God be-

75

come man, are at once tormenting and sweet; they are not an obstacle to a supernatural happiness. St. Bonaventure remarked of the Poverello that in him joy is transfigured to the point of tears. "I tremble with joy," said his sister Clare, "and I do not fear that anyone may rob me of such happiness."

Such is then the result of the message which the cloistered nun of St. Damian had to deliver to the world. Unlike her friend, she did not sing, her joy in God in sublime Canticles, she did not make joy radiate in these words, so luminous with poetry, which we carry in our hearts. But she also bore witness by other means, which were those of her vocation proper. In one of his letters to the saint the celebrated Cardinal Hugolino who, even before becoming pope, showed himself to be the most effective protector of the mendicant orders, evoked the radiance of the most moving of the virtues that we recognize in St. Clare: "Whence comes then this indescribable joy which sweeps over me when, in your presence and that of your sisters, we discoursed about the infinite love of the Lord? . . ." Clare, like Francis, must have intimated a tenderness, a joy and trust into this sublime colloquy which every contemplative soul holds with the ineffable Presence. And is it not true that in this beloved Umbria where she lived her life of prayer in this little convent, deliberately destitute of creature comforts, it is this secret joy, purer and more intense than any other, that we perceive, and we can still catch the echo of the words of love that welled up from within her heart?

6

Contemplation: an activity

Contemplation—Clare's inner splendor. Has one said everything, when one has tried to grasp—as if it were possible—this flame which burned at the heart of the virgin of Assisi, its reflection the gentle light radiating from her life? It is not enough to see this pure flame burn between the somber walls of the *conventino* at the foot of the hill, which she illumined with an inextinguishable light. It does not even suffice to look at it flaring in its own time, in a world threatened by bloody shadows, against which its lone presence rose to do combat. This lofty flame still burns among us after seven centuries, in the six hundred houses in which the daughters born of her spiritual works live according to her Rule.

This is one of the paradoxes of the epoch in which we live. This world which seems haunted by the demons of speed, of publicity and of profit, which recognizes as valid the principles of utility and enjoyment, is at the same time one in which many, very many men and women desire to live in the total immobility and silence of a life of renunciation which, according to the canons of the earth, serves no useful purpose. The baptized humanity of the twentieth century no longer supports itself, as did that of the twelfth and thirteenth century, on the indestructible foundations of a faith that nothing placed in doubt. But witnesses to this faith, which is perhaps more conscious, more lucid today for having been controverted and discussed, arise among us witnesses whose worth is not unequal to those in the time of St. Francis, of St. Dominic or of St. Bernard.

Everything has been said, and in all fields, about the "selfishness" and "uselessness" of the contemplative life. One must lose all sense of supernatural realities, and reduce religion to some kind of social mutual aid and propaganda enterprise, in order to admit for a second that a Poor Clare or a Carmelite is "less useful" than a nursing Sister or a daughter of St. Vincent de Paul. Such opinions reveal only this exaltation of an alleged real and of a self-styled utility which is the major heresy of the modern world. "Those who give themselves constantly to prayer and penance," wrote Pope Pius XI, "contribute to the progress of the Church and to the salvation of the human race even more effectively than those who cultivate the field of the Lord by their works of zeal." But perhaps such erroneous judgments, brought against a form of existence totally opposed to that of people of today, merely translate the tacit condemnation which the contemplative brings against them and their erring ways.

The true source of progress

78   It is not only by its value judgment and condemnation that *lived* contemplation imposes itself on us like a lesson. In this world, gripped by the frenzy and passion for

material things, a daughter of St. Clare in her monastery does more than set an example. She even does more than demonstrate, experimentally, that an existence of a totally different type is possible. In this existence all the energies that we would expend in the ceaselessly illusory and disappointed pursuit of a transitory happiness are used for the exaltation of the greatest qualities of man and carried out and realized in a perspective of eternity. Every soul which elevates itself, elevates the world as well, the poet has said. Merely by wanting to go beyond the requirements of human matter, to transcend its miseries and its connivances, the contemplative individual participates actively in a progress infinitely more authentic than the one that is counted in millions of automobiles or even in scientific discoveries.

This role, which we have seen the little saint of Assisi assume at the side of her friend engaged in harsher battles, this role of spiritual reserve, of a fund of grace and strength upon which the activist monks drew for assistance, is a role which is still theirs. It is a role which the closed universes of the convents still play apart from the violent world of men to which, however, they are linked by the thousand tendrils of prayer. How many men and women, launched upon hectic, over-hurried lives, feel the need to halt sometimes in these houses where all is silence, where time seems to be only the reflection of the non-temporal, and where a force which does not derive from the earth, but allows one the better to face its risks, imposes itself on the soul?

The prayer of the contemplative nun is not only the personal elevation and exaltation of the collective soul; it is a charity of sentiment and a gift of love. If her only aim is to adhere to God, to participate in his light, the effort alone that she accomplishes to attain it mysteriously shifts to the whole human community, according to the order of the communion of saints. The Christian is not a man alone: it is not by selfishness and isolation that he accomplishes his vocation. All things unite and pour forth again; each one is great only by virtue of others. This splendor which Clare, in her cell, pursued through vigils and penances was exactly that which shone on the face of Francis when he addressed crowds, standing on a public square. It is exactly the one which penetrated souls through the subterranean path of remorse and forgiveness. The silent prayer of a thousand communities, prisoners of their vows, works more effectively than all sermons to restore the soul, of which it is forgetful, to the Mystic Body of Christ—the Body which the Church of the baptized constitutes whether she wishes to or not—more efficaciously than all sermons.

God's lightning rods

Huysmans, speaking of the Carmelites, of the Carthusians and of the Trappists, in a beautiful phrase called them "God's lightning rods." But it is not only from the justified wrath of the Almighty that the nocturnal prayers and the sacrifices of the contemplative lives spare the earth. They spare us, just as much, from that wrath which rises within us and leaves a taste of disgust and bitterness on our lips when we think of this life of permanent infidelity and betrayal which we make ours by accepting it.

80   For it is in the course of life, in the hours of abandonment and misery in which the sole certainty of being only human rises in the gorge. Nothing seems to have meaning any more; everything is compromised, soiled, irremediably degraded. The strength and courage to look upon our body and our heart, without disgust of which Baudelaire speaks, is denied to us. Who am I? Why am I? And why am I such? Death insinuates its sarcastic shadow into this cruel meditation and into this infidel world which is ours, and it seems that the only aim to which it can legitimately aspire is nothingness. But it is then, when the temptation of despair and of the absurd harrows us that it is sweet to recall that there are places of safety, marked out on a map under the eye of the Father, where hope and love reign indestructible. The Christian's thoughts turn towards these beacons in order that their light may point out the road. And the lone certitude of far-off splendor suffices to restore peace of soul.

I am thinking of a house which I shall never visit, built on African earth, gleaming white under the harsh blue sky. I know about the life led there by the daughters of Clare, in holy poverty and in daily renunciation. The splendor which belonged to the radiant daughter of Assisi burns intact among them. And their fidelity never thinks of appealing to any other ideal than that of the first Damianites, the love of God become man, humble and constant obedience to the laws of the Gospel, charity, and sometimes joy, extended to the whole of humanity. In hours of solitude and weakness, my mind turns toward this distant dwelling where I know that, through prayer, my soul is not absent, hoping for help from it. And quite often, it has happened that in the deepest recesses of my being I have heard the hoped-for response, barely formulated but nonetheless explicit. This is what Francis must have read in Clare's eyes when, troubled over the road to follow or consumed by a secret torment, he would turn towards her, the meditative, the contemplative nun, the messenger of divine will. And in her look he drew upon a new strength with which to fight his daily battles anew.

7

St. Clare and St. Francis

We have collected here the principal texts, excerpted from the oldest Franciscan documents, dealing with the relations between the Poverello and St. Clare. The translation from the Italian is by Alexandre Masseron, in *La Légende Franciscaine*, Paris: Fayard.

How Clare came to know the blessed Francis and how she became friends with him

Since she heard much talk about Francis who, like a new man, wished to lead the world along the forgotten path of perfection by new virtues, Clare at once desired to see and hear him. She was prompted by the Holy Spirit of which both had already received the first fruits, although in different ways. And Francis, moved by the great fame of this gracious maiden, desired no less to see and speak with her to wrest this noble prey from the wicked world and to claim her for his Lord, for Him who had come to destroy the kingdom of this world which eagerly wanted to snatch his prize from Him. He visited her often, and she visited him even more often, choosing the times suitable for these visits in such a way that these divine relations might not be known by man or censured by public gossip. Accompanied only by one who enjoyed her trust and confidence, the girl often left her paternal home and held secret meetings with the man of God whose words seemed aflame and deeds superhuman. The blessed Father exhorted her to contempt of vainglory, pointing out to her in glowing terms how vain are earthly hopes and how deceptive worldly appearances. He counseled the sweetness of the nuptials of Christ to her, committing her to preserve the treasure of her virginity for the blessed Bridegroom whom love made man.

But why delay our account further? At the urging of the very holy father, who ingenuously played the role of a most loyal "best man," the girl was not long in giving her consent. Immediately, she was rapt in a contemplation of the eternal joys, the sight of which indeed made the world seem contemptible. Her desire for these joys uprooted her from her very being, and her love for them made her sigh longingly for the nuptials of heaven. Aglow with a celestial ardor, she now acquired such a lofty contempt of the show of earthly vanities, that nothing of that which wins the plaudits of the world entered her heart. Holding in horror the allurements of the flesh, she refused to know the defilement of her bed,[1] desiring to make of her body a temple for God alone, and striving by all her efforts to merit by her virtues to be the spouse of the Great King. She then submitted herself entirely to the guidance of Francis, considering him to be, after God, the director of her inner life. Thenceforth, her soul

86

[1] Wisdom 3:13.

clung to his holy teachings and she received, with an ardor-filled heart, everything which his words revealed to her about the gentleness of Jesus. Now she could only painfully bear the pomp and ornaments of the world, and she regarded all things which the world praises as dung,[2] in order to be able to gain Christ.[3]

How the blessed Francis led her out of the world and made her enter religion

So that the mirror of her spotless soul would not later be tarnished by the dust of the world nor her youth disturbed by the world's contagion, the very holy Father hastened to lead her out of this world of darkness. The solemn feast of Palm Sunday was at hand[4] when the girl, her heart afire, went to see the man of God to talk to him about her conversion and to ask when and under what conditions she should act. The blessed Francis ordered her to dress and adorn herself with finery on this feastday and go to receive the palms with the throng of other Christians, and on the following night to go forth outside the camp[5] and change her joy in the world into mourning[6] for the Passion of the Lord. When this Sunday arrived she entered the church with the people decked out in all her finery.

---

[2] Philippians, 3:8.
[3] *Légende de Sainte Claire Vierge*, (Assisi: F. Pennacchi, 1910), pp. 5–6.
[4] 1212, or, according to several historians, 1211.
[5] Hebrews, 13:3.
[6] James, 4:9.

The illustrations following

17. The road leading to St. Damian, lightly shaded by olive trees.

18. Holy poverty is present everywhere within St. Damian. Here, the nuns' choir.

19. The sanctuary is a place of special prayer and silence.

20. The refectory of the Poor Ladies—with its badly planed benches and cracked vaults.

21. An end of the dormitory has been furnished as an oratory.

22. From this side of the dormitory, we can see a cross; it marks the place where St. Clare died.

23. The most beautiful countenance ever given St. Clare is that painted by Simone Martini in the basilica of St. Francis, Assisi.

24. The cloister of St. Damian, where all is joy, peace and light.

Credits: (17, 21, 22, 24) Photo Léonard von Matt.
(18, 20) Photo Léonard von Matt from *Terres Franciscaines*, Plon.
(19) Photo published by Pietro-Vignati, Assisi.
(23) Photo Anderson-Giraudon.

17.

18.

19.

20.

22. ▲

23. ▶

By an admirable omen, as the others pressed forward to receive the palms and Clare out of modest shyness remained motionless in her place, the bishop, descending the steps, went up to her and placed the palm in her hand. On the following night, in accordance with the orders of the saint, she escaped as she had desired, with her virtuous companion. Since it seemed unwise to her to leave by the ordinary door, with her own hands and with an astonishing strength, she opened another which was blocked by piles of beams and stones.

Having thus abandoned her house, city and kinsmen, the virgin Clare fled hastily to St. Mary of the Porziuncola. Here she was received by the Friars, holding lighted torches, who were keeping a holy vigil in the little sanctuary of God. There, after casting aside the turpitudes of Babylon, she immediately issued the world a bill of divorce.[7] There, her tresses fell under the scissors wielded by the friars, and she bid farewell to her glittering adornments. It would not have been fitting that, in the evening of time, the order where virginity blossomed like a flower, should be born elsewhere than in the abode of her who was virgin and mother, the first and the highest in dignity among virgins. This is the place where the new militia of the poor had its first joyous beginnings under Francis' orders, so that it might be clearly manifest that the Mother of Mercy had desired to bring the two orders into the world in the hospitality of her dwelling. When the humble handmaid had received the livery of holy penance before the altar of the Blessed Mary and had been espoused to Christ, so to speak, before the bed of this same Virgin,

97

[7] Deut. 24:1.

St. Francis immediately led her to the church of St. Paul[8] so that she might remain there until the Most High should decide otherwise.[9]

The Poor Ladies: How the blessed Francis wanted the friars to conduct themselves with regard to them

It is not fitting to pass over in silence the remembrance of the spiritual edifice, much more precious than the material edifice which the blessed Francis, under the instigation of the Holy Spirit, erected in this place, after having repaired the stone church[10] to make the celestial church grow. It must not be thought that because he repaired a perishable building falling into ruin Christ spoke to him from the height of the Cross in such extraordinary manner that all those who knew of it were struck with fear and sorrow. But, just as the Holy Spirit[11] had predicted, one day an Order of holy virgins was to be instituted there, like a pile of living and well-cut stones who would be used to restore the abode of heaven. After the virgins of Christ had begun to gather at this place, to which they came from all parts of the world, and there

---

[8] At Bastia, near Assisi. It was a Benedictine monastery, from which, after a few days, Clare went to the convent of Sant'Angelo of Panzo, on the Subasio, also a Benedictine foundation. She remained there four months before establishing herself definitively at St. Damian where she died.

[9] Deut. 24:7–8.

[10] St. Damian.

[11] An allusion to a prophecy of St. Francis himself, relative to St. Damian and to the Poor Ladies, reported by Celano, *Seconde Légende,* I, VIII, 6.13.

attain the summit of perfection in the exercise of the greatest poverty and bathed in the radiance of all the virtues, the blessed father, little by little, deprived them of his bodily presence, even though he continued to take care of them and preserved all his affection towards them in the Holy Spirit. When they had given numerous proofs of this sovereign perfection and the saint assured himself that they were ready to endure all sacrifices and sufferings for Christ, and that they were resolved never to deviate from their holy observances, he firmly promised that he and his friars would always counsel and aid them and their sisters who would make a similar vow of poverty. He carefully kept this promise all during his life. And when death was at hand, he ordered that it always be thus. Said the blessed Francis: "It is the same spirit which led these friars and these Poor Ladies to leave the world."

Since the friars sometime were astonished that he did not let these holy handmaids of God enjoy his bodily presence more often, he replied: "Do not believe, beloved brothers, that I do not cherish them with all my affection. If I could be reproached for loving them in Christ, could I not be reproached even more for having united them to Christ? It would not have been contrary to righteousness not to have called them, but it would be inhuman not to be concerned about them after having called them. But it is an example that I give you so that you may act as I do myself. I do not want any of you spontaneously to offer to go visit them, but I do want truly spiritual men, tested by a long and holy religious life to be sent, despite them, to serve the needs of their souls."[12]

[12] Celano, *Seconde Légende*, II, CLV, pp. 204–205.

How the blessed Francis preached to them more by his example than by his words

During one of the holy father's visits to St. Damian, his vicar many times entreated him to bring the word of God to her daughters. Won over by her insistence, he consented thereto. So the Ladies gathered as usual to listen to the word of God, but with an equal desire to see their father. As for Francis, he looked up towards heaven, where his heart always dwelt, and began to preach Christ. Then he had some ashes brought to him, and spread part of them on the floor in a circle around him and placed the rest on his head. For a long time the blessed father remained silent within the circle of ashes, and at the sight of this a deep astonishment gripped the hearts of the waiting nuns. Suddenly he straightened up and to their ever increasing astonishment, he began to recite the *Miserere mei Deus* in the manner of a sermon. Upon finishing it, he immediately left the chapel.

This spectacle filled the handmaids of the Lord with such contrition that their tears flowed and they could barely keep from punishing themselves with their own hands. By his action he had taught them to consider themselves as ashes and to discard any feelings which would not be in perfect harmony with such an opinion.

Such were his relations with these holy women, of such a nature were his very useful, but brief and rare, visits. Thus it was his will that the friars serve the Poor Ladies, that in the name of Christ they serve themselves, but in such a way as to guard themselves, like birds, from falling into the traps that are always set.[13]

100

13 Celano, *Ibid*. CLVII, p. 207.

St. Francis and his companions
as well as St. Clare rapt in ecstasy

Francis, the servant of the Most High King, often comforted the blessed Clare by his holy exhortations, and she asked the blessed father to grant her the joy of taking his repast with her, at least once. But the blessed Francis always refused. But it happened that the holy father's companions learned of this wish of St. Clare and they said to the blessed father: "Father, it seems to us that this hardness with which you refuse to grant the wish of Sister Clare, this so holy virgin so beloved of God, does not conform to the divine will, since it was above all through your preaching that she abandoned the pomp of the world. Why do you not permit her just once to take her repast with you, since if she had asked you for a still greater favor, with such insistence you would have had to grant it to your little plant? St. Francis replied to them: "Hence you think I should grant her wish?" And they said, "Yes, indeed, Father, for she is worthy of the joy you might give her." St. Francis replied: "Since you are of this opinion, I accept it. But that her joy be all the greater, I wish the repast to take place at St. Mary of the Angels. She has been cloistered at St. Damian for a long time, so she will be glad to see St. Mary's again where her tresses were shorn and where she became the spouse of Our Lord Jesus Christ. It is there that we shall eat together in the name of the Lord."

So he chose the day when the blessed Clare was to come and join him and his companions. She came and at first, respectfully and humbly, she venerated the Blessed Virgin, *101* the mother of the Lord, then she reverently visited the entire friary. At the hour of the repast, the humble and divine Francis, according to his custom, had the table set on the ground. He, as well as the blessed Clare, sat down, and one of the companions of the holy father sat next to the companion of St. Clare. Then all the other companions took their place around this humble table. But hardly had the repast begun when St. Francis began to discourse about God with such sweetness and holiness, with such loftiness and so divinely that he himself, and St. Clare and her companion, and all the others that were at this poor table were rapt in ecstasy by the super-abundance of the grace of the Most High which descended upon them.

And as they were seated in this manner, rapt in ecstasy, their hands and eyes lifted up to heaven, it seemed to the people of Assisi and Bettona[14] and from the whole countryside that the church of St. Mary of the Angels and the whole friary, and the forest, which surrounded it at that time, were aflame and that an immense conflagration was raging. So the men of Assisi came running in a great haste to save the friary, because they firmly believed that everything was burning. But when they arrived at the friary, they saw that absolutely nothing had been damaged. They entered the grounds and saw the blessed Francis and St. Clare and all their companions, rapt in the Lord, seated around this humble table, but invested with the virtue of heaven. They then were certain that this fire was a divine fire which was consuming these men and women saints with the abundant consolations of the

14 A village facing Assisi. Perched on a height as Assisi is, it overlooks St. Mary of the Angels, on the plain below.

divine love. So they returned to their home greatly edi-
fied and reassured.

As for blessed Francis and St. Clare and the others,
their souls were so strengthened by such an abundance of
divine consolation that they barely, or not at all, touched
the material food. After which, St. Clare returned to
St. Damian. The sisters rejoiced greatly upon seeing her
again. For they had feared that St. Francis might have
sent her to direct another monastery, just as he had already sent her sister Agnes to Florence as abbess. Moreover, he had once said to St. Clare herself: "Be prepared,
if necessary, to go wherever I should send you." And like
a true daughter of obedience, she had replied, "Father,
I am ready to go wherever it will please you." And
St. Clare remained greatly consoled in the Lord.[15]

[15] *Actus Beati Francisci et sociorum eius,* XV; *The Little Flowers,*
XV, where the title is slightly different. *How St. Clare ate a meal
at Saint Mary of the Angels with St. Francis and his companions.*

8

The prayers of St. Clare

We are indebted for the translation of several prayers, which St. Clare has left behind, to our friends among the Poor Clares. The Blessing is read by the Abbess every Saturday in the refectory of all the monastaries before saying grace before the whole community, lying prostrate.

The blessing of St. Clare[1]

In the name of the Father and of the Son and of the Holy Spirit. Amen.

May the Lord bless you and keep you, and show his face to you and have mercy on you. May he turn his countenance towards you and give you peace.

I, Clare, unworthy handmaid of Jesus Christ, a little plant of our father Francis, sister and mother to you and all other Poor Sisters, beseech our Lord Jesus Christ through his mercy and through the intercession of his most holy Mother Mary, and of blessed Michael the Archangel and of all the saints of God to give and confirm to you his most holy blessing in heaven and on earth. *105*

[1] Translation from the Italian by a Poor Clare of Casablanca.

On earth, by increasing your number through his grace and his virtues among his servants and handmaids, in his Church militant.

In heaven by exalting you and glorifying you in his Church triumphant, among all his saints.

I bless you while I still live, and after my death, as much as I can and even more than I can, with all the blessing with which the Father of Mercies has blessed his sons and his daughters according to the spirit, and with which he will bless them in heaven and on earth. Amen.

Be full of love at all times for me, for your souls, and for all Sisters and always be diligent in the observance of what you have vowed to the Lord. May the Lord be with you always, and may you be always everywhere with Him. Amen.

The prayer composed by St. Clare in honor of the five wounds of our Lord Jesus Christ[2]

In honor of the wound in the right hand:

Praise and glory be given thee, O Lord Jesus, for the most holy wound in thy right hand. Through the sacred wound, forgive all the sins that I have committed against thee in thought, word and deed, by neglect in thy service, and by my self-indulgences, both waking or sleeping. Grant that I preserve a pious remembrance of thy death on the Cross and of thy sacred wounds, and that

106

[2] Translated from the Italian by the Religious Clares Colettines of Enghien (Belgium).

The prayers of St. Clare

I may testify to my gratitude by retracing them on my body, through mortification. Grant this to me, O thou who livest and reignest, world without end. Amen. *Our Father* and *Hail Mary*.

In honor of the wound in the left hand:

Praise and glory be given thee, O very gentle Jesus, for the holy wound in thy left hand. Through this wound, have mercy on me and remove from my heart all therein that displeases thee. Grant me victory over the relentless enemies who wage war against me. Fill me with thy strength so that I may trample upon them. Through thy merciful death, deliver me from all the dangers to which my life and salvation are exposed, and deign to make me worthy of sharing thy glory in thy kingdom, O thou who livest and reignest, world without end. Amen. *Our Father* and *Hail Mary*.

In honor of the wound in the right foot:

Praise and glory be given thee, O good Savior Jesus, for the very holy wound in thy right foot. Through this wound, grant that I merit my forgiveness by a penance proportioned to the magnitude of my sins. Oh! I beseech thee through thy death, to keep thy poor monastery continually united to thy will, and to preserve its body and soul from all adversity. When the dreadful day will have arrived, receive my soul into thy mercy and bequeath it eternal joys, O Lord who livest and reignest, world without end. Amen. *Our Father* and *Hail Mary*.

In honor of the wound in the left foot:

Praise and glory be given to thee, O very merciful Jesus, for the very holy wound in thy right foot. Through this sacred wound, grant me the grace of a full and complete indulgence, so that by thy help, O merciful Jesus, before dying, I may receive the sacrament of thy body and thy blood, by the confession of all my sins, with a perfect contrition and a complete purity of body and mind. Grant, finally, that I may receive the sacrament of Last Anointing, for eternal life. Hear my prayer, O Lord, who livest and reignest, world without end. Amen. *Our Father* and *Hail Mary*.

In honor of the wound in the side:

Praise and glory be given to thee, O most amiable Jesus, for the very holy wound in thy side. Through this sacred wound and through this immense mercy that thou hast shown in allowing that thy side be opened, and which thou showest for all our sakes, after having first shown it to the soldier Longinus, I beseech thee, most gentle Jesus, that it does not suffice thee to have purified me of original sin by baptism, but that thou further deignest to deliver me from all evils, past, present and future, through the merits of thy precious blood which now is offered and received in all the world. Through thy death, so full of bitterness, grant me a lively faith, an indestructible hope and a perfect charity, so that I may love thee with all my heart, with all my soul and with all my strength. Establish me in holy ways, so that I may persevere courageously in thy holy service, and that I may please thee now and always. Amen. *Our Father* and *Hail Mary*.

The prayers of St. Clare

We adore Thee, Jesus Christ, and we bless thee because by thy Holy Cross thou hast redeemed the world.
Let us pray.

O Almighty and Eternal God, who hast redeemed the human race through the five wounds of thy Son, Our Lord Jesus Christ, grant us, we beseech thee, that after having, each day, venerated these same wounds, that we may avoid a sudden and eternal death through the merits of thy blood and death. We beseech it through the same Lord Jesus who lives and reigns with thee, world without end. Amen.

9

The letters of St. Clare

Only five letters have been preserved from Clare's correspondence. They have been translated by Madeleine Havard de La Montagne at the end of the French edition of *The Life of St. Clare* by Thomas of Celano.

Letter to St. Ermentrude[1]

To Ermentrude, her dearest sister, Clare of Assisi, humble handmaid of Jesus Christ.

Health and peace!

I have learned, most dear sister, that with the help of God's grace, you have fled the defilement of the world: for this I rejoice and I congratulate you. And I rejoice again because you and your daughters are walking along the path of virtue. Dearest one, be faithful unto death to him to whom you have made your promises, for it is from him you shall receive the crown of life. Short are our labors here below, but the rewards are eternal. Do not let yourself be troubled by the tumult of the world which flits by like a shadow. May the vain phantoms of the

111

[1] Cf. Wadding, *Annales Minorum,* IV, pp. 80–81, XX.

deceptive world never confuse you. Close your ears to the promptings of hell, and frustrate its efforts with all your might.

Bear adversities cheerfully and let not prosperity lift you up: the former calls for faith, the latter requires it. Render faithfully what you have vowed to God: he shall reward you. O dear one, look up at the heaven which calls us, take up the cross and follow Christ who walks ahead of us. After the many and numerous tribulations, he will introduce us to his glory. Love God with all your heart, and also his son Jesus, crucified for us. May the remembrance of him never leave your mind. Meditate constantly on the mysteries of the Cross and on the sorrows of his Mother at the foot of the Cross. Ever pray and keep watch at all times. Carry out the work that you have begun actively, and discharge the ministry of your choice in holy poverty and in sincere humility. Fear not, my daughter! God, faithful in all his words and holy in all his works will shower his blessings upon you and your daughters. He will be your aid and your best consolation. He is our Redeemer and our eternal reward.

Let us pray to God for each other. By thus carrying the burden of charity from one to the other, we may easily follow the law of Christ. Amen.

The first letter to blessed Agnes of Bohemia[2]

To the illustrious and venerable virgin Agnes, daughter of the most powerful and ever invincible King of Bohemia.

112 Clare, unworthy servant of Jesus Christ and handmaid

[2] Cf. *Acta Sanctorum*, Martii, I, pp. 505–507.

of the virgins consecrated to God in the monastery of St. Damian, offers her spiritual services and, with the most humble deference, and beseeches the glory of eternal happiness on her behalf! I have heard about your holy deeds and the glory of your irreproachable life, which has not come only to our attention, but to that of almost all the world. I am transported with joy and happiness in the Lord, like all those whose desire is to fulfill the will of Jesus Christ and to be agreeable to him, or who already fulfill it.

We know how you could have prevailed over all others in enjoying the honors and glory of this world and become even the spouse of the most august of Caesars, as was fitting to His and Your Majesty. With all the affection of your heart, impelled by a keen desire, you have preferred holy poverty and the mortification of the flesh. You have united yourself with a much more noble Spouse, with Our Lord Jesus Christ himself. He will keep your pure and stainless virginity inviolable always. 'Whom when you have loved, you are chaste; Whom when you have touched you are purer yet, Whom when you have taken to yourself, you are a virgin; Whose power is stronger, Whose nobility higher, Whose countenance is more beautiful, and love more tender and courtesy more pleasing. In his embrace you are already caught up, and he has adorned your breast with precious stones and set priceless pearls in your ears, and girded you round with glorious and shining gems and crowned you with a golden crown on which is engraven holiness.'[3]

Thus, dearest sister, nay, mistress venerable because you

[3] Several phrases in this paragraph occur in the office of St. Agnes, Roman Breviary.

are the spouse, mother and sister of my Lord Jesus Christ, adorned with the glorious standard of incorruptible virginity and holy poverty, strengthen yourself in the holy service into which you have entered, animated by a burning desire after the example of Jesus Christ, the Poor One. He suffered cruel torments on the Cross for us all; he has delivered us from the tyranny of the Prince of Darkness, of whom the sin of our first parent made us prisoners, and he has reconciled us to God the Father. O blessed Poverty! to those who possess you is given the kingdom of the heavens, eternal glory is promised and the blessed life infallibly granted. O lovable Poverty! Our Lord, who ruled and now rules heaven and earth who spoke and things were made embraced you! It is he who says, "The foxes have dens, and the birds of the air have nests; but the Son of Man, Christ, has nowhere to lay his head," "but bowing his head, he gave up his spirit." Thus a Lord so great and good, upon entering into the spotless virgin's womb, willed to be born in this world poor. And men, poor and lacking the bread of life, have through him become rich and masters of the celestial kingdom.

Be glad, then, and abandon yourself to the transports of happiness; overflow with spiritual joy! You have preferred the contempt of this world to its honors, poverty to temporal riches, the treasures of heaven to those of the earth. You have been judged worthy to become the spouse and mother of the Son of the Most High and of the glorious Virgin Mary. I am assured by a faith most firm that you believe and know that the kingdom is promised only to the poor, and that Our Lord will grant it only to the poor. To love the things of this world is to lose the

114

fruit of love. It is impossible to serve God and Mammon; either we love the one and hate the other, or either we serve the one and despise the other. You know this too: that one clothed cannot fight with one naked; one cannot struggle against the world adorned with garments because he who gives his enemy a chance to hold him is lost in advance. It is difficult to live with pomp in this world and to reign with Christ in the other. A camel would pass more easily through the eye of a needle than a rich man would enter the kingdom of heaven. You have rejected the garments, I mean the world's riches. Thus your victory in the struggle against its wiles will be more certain, and you will enter the kingdom of heaven by the narrow way. Assuredly a felicitous exchange and worthy of all praise, to leave earthly goods for eternal blessings, to gain the goods of heaven at the cost of the things of earth, to receive a hundred-fold in place of one and to enjoy the blessed life. Therefore I have resolved to beseech Your Highness and Your Holiness by humble prayers, in the bosom of Jesus Christ, to strengthen yourself in his holy service, to progress from good to better, from virtue to virtue. May he, whose handmaid you wish to be with all your heart, deign to adorn you with all the abundance of his grace. I beseech you also in the name of the Lord and with all my might, that in your holy prayers you commend to God me, your unworthy handmaid, and the other Sisters who are with me in this monastery. With the help of your prayers we may merit the mercy of Jesus Christ so that with you, we shall be worthy of enjoying the vision eternal. Farewell in the Lord. Pray for me. *Alleluia.*

115

The second letter to blessed Agnes

To the daughter of the king of kings, to the virgin of virgins. To the most worthy bride of Jesus Christ and to Queen Agnes: Clare, the useless and unworthy handmaid of the poor virgins: health and perseverance in living in the greatest poverty!

I render thanks to the author of grace and to him from whom we believe comes every good gift and every perfect gift. He has embellished you with so many virtues and has led you to such perfection so that by imitating the perfection of the Father you may be worthy of becoming perfect so that his eyes may see nothing imperfect in you. Such is the perfection whereby the King of Heaven will unite you to himself in the eternal joys where he dwells gloriously on a star-studded throne. You have despised the noble honors of an earthly kingdom, and disdained the delights of an imperial marriage. You have become the lover of poverty, and, in a spirit of great humility and ardent love you have cleaved to the footprints of Jesus, and have been judged worthy of being united to him in marriage.

I have known that all the virtues abound in you, so I shall not weary you with a long discourse even though, perhaps, to you nothing in these matters, from which some consolations may come into being, may seem superfluous. One thing is needful, however, and I only suggest it: for the love of him to whom you have offered the sweet sacrifice of your person, I exhort you to be mindful of your vocation, like another Rachel. Never lose sight of the beginning. Hold on to what you now possess, do well what you are now doing. Never linger on the road; on

116

the contrary, advance joyously and securely along the path of so great an honor, swiftly and with light and peaceful step that raises no dust. Trust no one, consent to no one who would deflect you from your resolution and restrain your course. Run to the perfection to which the spirit of God calls you: there, you will fulfill your vows to the Most High and your steps along the path of God's commandments will be more secure. You will follow the counsels of our Reverend Father, Brother Elias, Minister General of all our Order. You must resolve to follow them in preference to all others and you must hold them to be more precious than any other gift. If anyone tells you, or suggests to you, something opposed to your perfection and the vocation to God, even though you might be glorified and honored by it more than any other man, follow not his counsels, but as a poor virgin embrace the poor Christ. Contemplate him who became despised for you, follow him, you who have also become despised in this world.

O illustrious Queen, behold your Spouse: the most beautiful of the sons of men became the ugliest of men for your salvation, his body torn and rent by scourgings. He expired on the Cross in extreme suffering. May your whole heart burn with a desire to imitate him! If you suffer with him, you shall be glorified with him. Sharing his sorrows, you shall share his joys. Remain on the Cross, and you shall have your place in the celestial abode, among the glory of the saints. Your name will be inscribed in the Book of Life, to be called glorious hereafter. In place of the transitory things of this world you will receive eternal goods, and you shall live in a state of happiness forever. Farewell, very dear sister and virgin, blessed because of your Spouse. Remember to commend me and my sisters, who are transported with joy at the sight of the good things with which God gratifies you, to the Lord. Commend us also to your sisters.

The third letter to blessed Agnes

To the honorable virgin in Jesus Christ above all others.

To sister Agnes, dearer than any other mortal, daughter of the illustrious King of Bohemia, now spouse and sister of the sovereign King of Heaven.

Clare, humble and unworthy servant of God, handmaid of the poor virgins, wishes you the joy of salvation in the Author of salvation, and all good things that can be desired!

Your good health, constancy and continual progress in your happy enterprise and, I understand, your joyous perseverance in the pursuit of celestial reward fill my heart with a lively joy in the Lord. The cause of my joy is that I see that by imitating the humility and the poverty of Jesus Christ, you make up for the insufficiency of my sisters and myself in this precious imitation. Truly, I have a good right to rejoice, nor can anyone rob me of this joy. The object of my desires under heaven is in your possession. Do I not see you, with an admirable prudence and wholly enveloped by the grace of God, triumph over the wiles of the enemy, of pride and of vanity which leads the hearts of men to perdition and madness? Do I not see you prefer the treasure, hidden in the field of this world and in the heart of men, of such great value in the eyes of him who created all from nothing? You enjoy the humiliations of virtue, of faith and of poverty. And, to

118

borrow the words of the apostle, you are, I affirm, the helper of God himself and the failing members of his infallible body are supported and reanimated by you. Who then would prevent me from rejoicing over such great goods? Rejoice also always in the Lord, my dearest one, and let no bitterness affect you.

O virgin, most beloved in Christ, joy of the angels and crown of your sisters! Fix your mind on the mirror of eternity, place your soul in the splendor of glory, attach your heart to the features of divine substance and by dint of contemplating God transform your whole self into the image of God. You will have the feelings of his friends, you will taste the secrets of his sweetness. At first Almighty God hides them from his friends as he does from all those who, in this deceitful and ensnaring world of men, blindly seized by their own selves, forsake him during their life. Love him with all your heart; with all your heart. He gave himself up out of love for you. The sun and the moon admire his beauty, the greatness and abundance of his reward are without limits. Love, I say, this Son of God, Most High. A virgin bore him and she remained a virgin after giving birth. Cling to the most sweet Mother who begot a Son whom the heavens were powerless to contain. She carried him in the frail womb of her little body, and held him to her maidenly breast. Who would not have risen up with indignation upon seeing the snares of vainglory and passing pomp with which the enemy of the human race works to bring to naught what is greatest in heaven. Through the grace of God I am convinced that the most worthy creature, the soul of a faithful man is greater than heaven. The heavens and all the other creatures could not contain the Creator, yet

119

The illustrations following

25. *The little terrace of the convent of St. Damian where Clare came to sit and meditate.*

26. *St. Clare with lilies, detail of a painting by Tiberus of Assisi in the basilica of St. Mary of the Angels.*

27. *The cemetery of St. Damian and its guard of cypress.*

28. *Pope Innocent IV, several cardinals and brownfriars, and a great crowd attended the funeral of St. Clare, August 12, 1253. A detail of the fresco attributed to Puccio Capanna which adorns the church of St. Clare.*

29. *The doorway of the cell in St. Damian where Clare's youngest sister died. Sister Agnes, as she was called, had, like Clare, fled her father's house to consecrate herself to God.*

30. *This admirable Crucifixion venerated at St. Damian was sculpted in wood in 1638 by Brother Innocent of Palermo.*

31. *A curious representation of St. Clare in an unimaginably severe old age. A painting by Vivarini in the Academy of Fine Arts, Venice.*

 Credits: (25, 29, 30) Photo Léonard von Matt.
(26, 28, 31) Photo Alinari-Giraudon.
(27) Photo Jean-Marie Marcel.

26.

28.

31.

a faithful soul becomes his habitation and his throne, and
this through the charity of which the impious are deprived. Truth has said: "Who loves me will be loved by
my Father, and I shall love him and we will come to him
and make our abode with him." The glorious Virgin of
Virgins carried the God become Man in her virginal
womb. You also, by imitating his humility and his
poverty, you will always be able to carry and contain him
who contains all things. You and the others who will
have despised the riches of the world, will possess him
more fully. Some kings and queens here below delude
themselves in this: even if their pride should mount to
heaven, and if their heads were to touch the summit,
they would no less end as dung-heaps.

Now I come to the points about which you asked my
opinion. On what feasts are we allowed to change our
food? Here they are transcribed for your charity in the
manner that our holy father Francis bade us to celebrate
them. Here, then, is what he says:

"Excepting the infirm and the sick (he asks, and even
commands that one strain one's ingenuity in providing
them with a varied fare) some of us are allowed, providing that we enjoy good bodily health, to take other food
than those served at Lent, both on ferial days or feasts.
Fast is obligatory every day, except Sunday and Christmas.
On these days there are two repasts, as well as on ordinary
Thursdays. Each is free to share therein, and a sister who
does not think it good to fast is not obliged thereto."

Because of our good health we fast every day, except
Sundays, Christmas and the whole of Easter week as the
Rule of our father St. Francis teaches us. Likewise, fasting *129*
is not obligatory on the feasts of the holy Virgin and of

the holy apostles, unless they fall on Friday. As I have said, because we are well and able, we always partake of the Lenten fare. However, our body is not made of brass and our strength is not that of stones. Our frailty, on the contrary, subjects us to bodily infirmities, so I ardently beseech you in the Lord to forbid yourself this overly strict abstinence that I know you practice. Live and hope in the Lord, and may your service be in accordance with reason. Season your sacrifice with the salt of prudence!

Farewell in the Lord, according to your desire. Commend me and my sisters to your holy sisters.

The fourth letter to blessed Agnes

To the illustrious Queen Agnes, who is half of my soul, the shrine of my special love, to my very dear mother and daughter beloved above all. Clare, the unworthy servant of Christ and the useless handmaid of the handmaids living in the monastery of St. Damian: health and the joy of singing with other virgin saints before the throne of God and the Lamb, and to follow the Lamb wherever he goes.

O mother and daughter, spouse of the King of Ages, do not be astonished that I have not written you as often as both my soul and yours desire it. Do not ever believe for a moment that the fire of love with which I burn for you has cooled in the slightest. Your mother loved you with all her heart, and I love you as she did. There is only one obstacle, few messengers and the great perils of the roads. Today brings the opportunity to write you: I rejoice with you and I share your joy in the Holy Spirit, bride of Christ. The first St. Agnes was espoused to the spotless

Lamb who takes away the sins of the world. To you also, blessed one, he has given the celestial union of this marriage which stunned with admiration the heavenly hosts. All desire him: whose remembrance assuages, whose goodness fills us to overflowing, whose fragrance revives the dead and whose glorious vision blesses all the inhabitants of heavenly Jerusalem. He is the splendor of glory, the brightness of eternal light, the mirror without spot. Look into that mirror daily, O Queen and spouse of Jesus Christ. Contemplate your face often therein so that within and without you may be adorned with the greatest variety of virtues like so many flowers, and arrayed in the garments that become the daughter and the spouse of the Most High King. Dearest beloved, on looking into that mirror, with the grace of God, you will be able to savor delights. Approach it and you will see there first Jesus asleep in the crib, his extreme poverty, his miserable swaddling clothes. O astounding poverty! O marvelous poverty! The King of the Angels, the Lord of Heaven and Earth, lying in a manger! In the middle of this mirror, behold the blessed poverty of holy humility. For the redemption of the human race, it made him endure untold sufferings and hardships.

In the end of the mirror, finally, contemplate the ineffable love which drove him to suffer on the wood of the Cross and to die there the most shameful death. This mirror, attached to the tree of the Cross, called the passers-by with these words: "All ye that pass by the way, attend, and see if there be any sorrow like to my sorrow." Let us respond to his cry and lamentation with one voice and one mind: "I will be mindful and remember, and my soul shall languish within me." Burn with this ardent love, O Queen, and recall also the unutterable delights of your celestial King, his riches and eternal honors. Give expression to your keen desire, and in your deep love, cry out: "Draw me after thee: we will run to the odor of thy ointments, O heavenly bridegroom! I will run and faint not, until thou bring me into the cellar of wine, until thy left hand to be under my head and thy right hand happily embrace me, and thou kiss me with the kiss of thy mouth!"

Pause to consider this, remember your poor mother. Know that your sweet remembrance is indelibly written on the tablet of my heart, since you are the dearest among all.

What more can I say! Let the tongue of my flesh be silent on the subject of my love for you. Words are the language of the mind, blessed daughter: the love that I feel for you is beyond bodily language. Hence, though my letter is not the equal of my love, receive it with benevolence and goodness. Behold in it, at least, the mark of the maternal love with which I burn every day for you and your daughters. Commend us, my daughters and myself, to them, dear, most worthy Agnes.

Farewell, dearly beloved, to you and your daughters, pray for us unto the throne of glory of the great God.

With all my power I recommend to your charity these messengers whom we have dispatched to you, our very dear brothers, Brother Amato, beloved of God and men, and Brother Bonaugura.

10

The testament of St. Clare

The most moving document of St. Clare that we possess is the Testament which she wrote to bequeath her spiritual lessons to her daughters. When they read it the Poor Clares preface it with an "eulogy" which magnifies its significance.

Praises of the testament[1]

Testament of peace, testament which must never fall into oblivion nor be held in disdain, nor changed by a contrary will! O Testament which has been confirmed, I say, not by the death of the testator but by the gift of immortal life.

Blessed be the one who disdains not, and never rejects the incorruptible Testament of charity, the fertile soil of humility, the desirable treasure of poverty, the precious legacy of so great and good a Mother!

The testament

In the Name of Our Lord, Amen.

Among the many graces which we have already re- *133*

[1] Translated from the Italian by a Poor Clare of Casablanca.

ceived and which we receive still every day from the liberality of the Father of Mercies, and for which we glorify him by giving our deepest thanks, the principal grace is our vocation. And we are all the more grateful for it, because it is the greatest and the most perfect of them.

Hence the apostle says: "Know your vocation."

The Son of God became for us the Way, which our blessed father Francis has shown and taught to us by word and example.

Therefore, beloved sisters, we must consider the immense benefits with which God has showered us, and especially those which he has deigned to work in us through his beloved servant, our blessed father Francis, those that he bestowed upon us not only after our conversion but already when we still lived among the vanities of the world.

The saint himself did not yet have either friars or companions. It was almost immediately after his conversion when he was repairing the church of St. Damian, where after a visitation by the Lord and being filled with his consolations, he was led to abandon the world wholly. It was then, in the transports of a holy joy and in the splendor of the Holy Spirit, that he uttered that prophecy concerning us which the Lord later fulfilled. For after having mounted the wall of this church, and addressed himself to some poor folk of the neighborhood, he said to them in a loud voice in French, "Come, help me to build the monastery of St. Damian, for it will be the dwelling of Ladies whose fame and holy life will glorify the Heavenly Father throughout his holy Church."

134

We can behold in this, therefore, the immense goodness

of God toward us. For it is through the superabundance of his mercy and of his love that he deigned to have his saint speak thus of our vocation and election. And it was not of us alone that our blessed father prophesied these things, but of others also who were to follow us in this holy vocation to which the Lord has called us. How great, therefore, must be our solicitude and fervor of mind and body for us to fulfill the commandments of God and of our Father so that we may return to him, after we have increased it, the talent which he has given us.

The Lord, in fact has placed us as an example, as models and mirrors, not only for other faithful but also for our sisters whom he has called to the same vocation, so that in turn they may be mirrors and models for those living in the world.

The Lord, therefore, has called us to such great things so that our sanctity should serve as a model and as a mirror in which even those who are models and mirrors for others may behold themselves. Consequently we are truly bound to bless and praise the Lord and to be strengthened more and more in him so that we may do good.

Wherefore, by living in accordance with the present Rule, we shall leave a noble example to others, and through a labor of short duration we shall gain the prize of eternal bliss.

After the Most High Heavenly Father, through his mercy and grace, had deigned to illumine my heart and inspire me to do penance, according to the example and following the teaching of our blessed father Francis, shortly after his conversion, in concert with some sisters whom God had given to me soon after my conversion, I voluntarily put my vow of obedience into his hands, according to the light and the grace which the Lord had granted us by the holy life and the teaching of his servant.

The blessed Francis perceived that we were weak and fragile of body, but that nevertheless neither hardship, poverty, work, tribulation and ignominy, nor the contempt of the world, in short that nothing of all this made us retreat. Rather he saw that all these things seemed to be unutterable delights, after the example of his friars and saints. Indeed, he and his friars often remarked this and rejoiced greatly in the Lord.

Wherefore, impelled by a surge of fatherly affection for us, he pledged himself and promised that he in his own person and through his Order would have a diligent care and a special solicitude for us.

Thus by the will of God and our blessed father Francis, we came to dwell at the church of St. Damian. There in a short time the Lord, by his grace and mercy, increased our number so that what had been foretold through His holy servant might come to pass. Before that we had sojourned at another place, but briefly.

Afterwards St. Francis prescribed a form of life for us, above all so that we might persevere always in holy poverty. During his life he was not content to exhort us often, by words and example, to the love and observance of most holy poverty, for he also bequeathed us many writings so that after his death we would never turn aside from it in any way.

And I, Clare, who though unworthy, am the handmaid of Christ and of the poor sisters of the monastery of St. Damian and the little plant of the holy patriarch, have with my sisters given consideration to our most high

136

calling and the command of so great and good a father, and also the frailty of others, fearing for ourselves after the death of our father St. Francis, who was our pillar, and after God our only consolation and our support.

Therefore, we have several times voluntarily renewed our vow to our Lady, most holy Poverty, so that after my death the sisters present and to come may never in any way abandon her.

And since I myself have always taken diligent care and solicitude to observe and have others observe holy poverty, which we have promised to the Lord and to our father Francis, so the other abbesses who shall succeed me in my office are bound always to observe and have it observed by their sisters unto the end.

In addition, for greater surety, I had recourse first of all to Pope Innocent,[2] whose pontificate witnessed the beginning of our Institute and then to his successors, and I had our profession of most holy poverty confirmed and strengthened by their pontifical privilege.

Wherefore, on bended knee and prostrated in body and soul at the feet of our Holy Mother, the Roman Church, and of the Sovereign Pontiff, and especially of the Lord Cardinal, who is assigned to the Order of the Friars Minor and to us, I commend all my sisters present and to come. And for the love of Jesus, who was so poor in his crib, who was so poor during his life, and who hung naked on the Cross, for love of him, I pray the Cardinal to protect this little flock which the Most High Heavenly Father has begotten in the holy Church through the word and example of the blessed father Francis, imitator of the poverty and of the humility of the Son of God and of the

137

[2] Innocent III.

glorious Virgin, his Mother; I pray the Cardinal to preserve this flock and to encourage it always in the observance of the holy poverty that we have promised to
God and to our blessed father Francis.

And since the Lord has given us our blessed father
Francis as founder, father and support in the service of
Christ and in our promises to God and to this blessed
father who placed so much diligence in his words and
works to foster the growth of us his plants. Now, in my
turn, I commend my sisters, present and to come, to the
successor of our blessed father Francis, and to the friars
of all his Order, so that they will aid us in ever pro-
gressing in the good and in the better service of God,
and above all in the better observance of most holy
poverty.

And if it should ever come to pass that my sisters should
leave this place and be transferred elsewhere, let them
nevertheless be bound, wherever they may be after my
death, to the observance of the same form of poverty as
we have promised God and our blessed father Francis.

But let her who will be in my office and the other
sisters ever show the care and prudence not to acquire or
accept land around their dwelling except for the strict
necessity of a vegetable garden.

And if at some time, for the proper convenience and
seclusion of the monastery it is further necessary to
acquire land outside the precincts of the garden, that they
do not permit the acquisition of more of it than required
by sheer need, and that this land be neither ploughed, nor
sown, and that it always remain uncultivated and un-
touched.

I admonish all my sisters, present and to come, and I

138

exhort them in Our Lord Jesus Christ always to strive to follow the way of holy simplicity, of humility and of poverty, and to live worthily and holily just as we have been taught from the beginning of our conversion to Jesus Christ by our blessed father Francis. Thus with these virtues, not acquired through our merits, but through the mercy and grace alone of our benefactor, the Father of Mercies, the sisters may spread the fragrance of a good name for all the others, for those sisters who are far and for those who are near.

And in the love of Christ love one another, and show the love that you have within you outwardly by your works, so that such an example may inspire the sisters to grow always in the love of God and in mutual charity.

I also beseech the sister who shall be entrusted with the guidance of the sisters to govern them more by her virtues and the holiness of her life, than by the dignity of her office, so that the sisters, inspired by her example, will obey her not only out of duty, but rather out of love.

In addition, let her show the discretion and solicitude of a good mother for her daughters, and above all provide all of them with the alms given by the Lord, giving to each according to her need. Let her also be so kind and so approachable to all, that they may disclose their needs to her with surety and have recourse to her with confidence, as they may deem necessary for themselves or for their sisters.

For their part the sisters subject to her should remember that they have renounced their wills for God's sake.

Therefore, I will that they obey their mother, with a spontaneous will, as they have promised the Lord, so that this mother, seeing the charity, humility and the unity

139

that reigns among them, may bear the burden of her duties more lightly, and their holy life may change what is painful and bitter into sweetness for her.

How strait is the way that leads to life! And how narrow is the gate through which one must enter! Thus there are few who walk along this path and who pass through this gate. And if there are some who walk along the path for a moment, O how rare are those who know how to persevere there!

But happy are those to whom it is given to walk thereon and to persevere unto the end!

And, after having entered upon the way of the Lord, let us watch never to turn aside from it in any manner through our own fault, negligence or ignorance. This would be to do injury to so great a Lord, the Virgin, his Mother, our blessed Francis and the Church triumphant, and finally the Church militant.

Now, it is written, "Cursed are they who turn aside from thy commandments."

For this reason I bend my knees before the Father of Our Lord Jesus Christ, so that, through the prayers and merits of the glorious and holy Virgin, his Mother, and those of our blessed father Francis and of all the saints, the Lord himself who has given us a good beginning will also give us increase and perseverance to the end. Amen.

I leave this writing to you, my dearest and most beloved sisters, present and to come. May it be a sign of the blessing of the Lord and of our blessed father Francis and of the blessing that I, who am your mother and handmaid, impart to you.[3]

140

[3] *Seraphicae Legislationis, textus originales,* pp. 273–280.

Selected bibliography

Ainsi parlait saint François. Paris: 1955. *A miscellany compiled by Franciscans.*

Goulven, J., *Rayonnement de sainte Colette.*

L'Histoire abregée de l'Ordre de Sainte-Claire, by the Abbess of the Poor Clares of Lyons. Paris: 1906. *Very detailed.*

La Montagne, M. Havard de, trans., *Thomas de Celano's La Vie de sainte Claire.* Paris: 1917. *This French translation is the base of all the documentation on Clare of Assisi.*

Mauclair, Camille, *La Vie de sainte Claire d'Assise.* Paris: 1927. *Unquestionably the most vivid account of the saint's life.*

Masseron, Alexandre, *La Légende Franciscaine.* Paris: 1954.

The author and his book

HENRI DANIEL-ROPS *is the nom de plume of Henri Jules Charles Petiot, born January 19, 1901, in France. Young Petiot, the son of an artillery officer, majored simultaneously in law, geography and history, winning the equivalent of a Masters degree in each before he was twenty-one years old. Within the year he accepted the post of Associate Professor of History. He retired from a teaching career as Professor of History at Neuilly in 1945.*

The name Daniel-Rops first appeared on a volume of essays published in 1926. Since that time Daniel-Rops has written more than seventy books, novels, poetry, children's books and historical studies. He has been honored for his work by election to the Académie Française and has won the Grand Prix of the Académie. Other honors conferred include Commander of the Order of St. Gregory the Great, by Pope Pius XII; the Grand Cross by Pope John XXIII; Grand Officer of the Order of Christ; and Officer of the Legion of Honor.

In this country his greatest successes have been This is the Mass, Jesus and His Times *and* Daily Life in the Time of Jesus. *Currently he is editor-in-chief of The Twentieth Century Encyclopedia of Catholicism, a 150-volume enterprise to which he has contributed a much-acclaimed volume. Daniel-Rops also contributes regularly to many French magazines and newspapers, edits a popular monthly journal,* Ecclesia, *and publishes a learned quarterly.—Some of his published works in English are:* Misted Mirror (*Knopf, 1931*); Two Men and Me (*Rockwell, 1931*); The Poor and Ourselves (*Burns, Oates & Washbourne, 1938*); Jesus and His Times

143

(*Dutton, 1954*); This Is the Mass (*Hawthorn, 1958*); What Is the Bible? (*Hawthorn, 1958*); Heroes of God (*Hawthorn, 1959*); The Book of Mary (*Hawthorn, 1960*); Monsieur Vincent (*Hawthorn, 1961*); Sources of the Life of Christ, *Daniel-Rops et al.* (*Hawthorn, 1962*); The Second Vatican Council (*Hawthorn, 1962*); Daily Life in the Time of Jesus (*Hawthorn, 1962*).

THE CALL OF ST. CLARE (*Hawthorn, 1963*) *was completely manufactured by The Book Press, Brattleboro, Vermont. The text type is Granjon, designed for the Linotype under the supervision of George W. Jones. It is named after Robert Granjon, the French type designer.*

A HAWTHORN BOOK

144